How to Make Your Own Video or Short Film

If you want to know how...

Learning to Read Music
*How to make sense of those mysterious symbols
and bring music alive*

Touch Typing in Ten Hours
Spend a few hours now and gain a valuable skill for life

How to Write for Television

howtobooks

Send for a free copy of the latest catalogue to:

How To Books
Spring Hill House, Spring Hill Road, Begbroke
Oxford OX5 1RX. United Kingdom.
email: info@howtobooks.co.uk
www.howtobooks.co.uk

How to Make Your Own Video or Short Film

All you need to know to make your ideas shine

BOB HARVEY

howtobooks

For Jane, James and Sarah

Published by How To Books Ltd,
Spring Hill House, Spring Hill Road,
Begbroke, Oxford OX5 1RX. United Kingdom.
Tel: (01865) 375794. Fax: (01865) 379162.
info@howtobooks.co.uk
www.howtobooks.co.uk

British Library Cataloguing in Publication Data
A catalogue record for this book is available from the British Library

ISBN 978 1 84528 256 1

Cover design by Baseline Arts Ltd, Oxford
Produced for How To Books by Deer Park Productions, Tavistock, Devon
Typeset by PDQ Typesetting, Newcastle-under-Lyme, Staffs.
Printed and bound by Bell & Bain Ltd, Glasgow

NOTE: The material contained in this book is set out in good faith for general guidance
and no liability can be accepted for loss or expense incurred as a result of relying in
particular circumstances on statements made in the book. The laws and regulations are
complex and liable to change, and readers should check the current position with the
relevant authorities before making personal arrangements.

Contents

Preface

Film-making has been both my passion and my career for almost 40 years. There can be few other pursuits that extend to us such an opportunity to express ourselves with the same kind of freedom and creative vigour, and it is no surprise that within the last few years new technologies have offered accessibility to the medium of video and film for virtually anyone who feels they have something to say. For me, picking up a camera, recording a series of events, then shuffling the scenes around in an edit suite to give an honest but creative interpretation of the original raw footage is not only supremely rewarding but one of the great joys of life, and one that everybody should try at least once.

The students I teach on my film course come from all walks of life, are of varying ages, nationalities and beliefs, and bring with them a wide range of subject matter they are keen to tackle, be it just for fun, for personal fulfilment or for a more serious career change.

Performers who feel compelled to show off their skills; charity workers who want to highlight the plight of the less fortunate; artists and writers eager to experiment within an audio visual medium; journalists keen to use film to explore social issues such as mental illness or threats to our freedom of speech; workers in uninspiring jobs who want to step into a world of discovery and challenge, and learn new skills along the way, or people who live in ordinary streets in ordinary towns who simply want to record and document events as they happen around them.

Once just the domain of professional film-makers, the door is now open to anyone with the will and creative integrity to produce a body of work, small or large, that can offer personal fulfilment whilst informing, inspiring and entertaining millions of people worldwide.

Acknowledgements

My thanks to David Hannah and Christian Bauer for introducing me to the delights and rewards of tutoring film students; to Jonny Persey and Luke Montagu at the Met Film School for their encouragement and support; Nikki Read and Giles Lewis at How To Books for the opportunity to document and share my experiences; Peter Appleyard for his technical advice; Andy Frost and Dan Haddon at Anglia Television for casting an experienced eye over my technical summaries, and Richard Crafter and Keith Judge for lending their camera and editing expertise respectively. My thanks also to Jane for her boundless enthusiasm, help and advice, Birta Bjargardottir for letting me take her dream concept and reworking it as *Dream World* – and to all the thousands of film-makers, past and present, amateur and professional, whose combined efforts have left a remarkable legacy for the film-makers of the future.

The Wonders of Choice

Today's emerging film-makers have unprecedented opportunities to make their mark. Never before has there been such choice in terms of subject matter and the means at their disposal to craft a story that can inspire, inform, educate and alter our perceptions of the world around us. Many may start by making small personal video diaries, or short experimental films, but once the bug takes hold you will invariably want to make bigger and better films and look for ways to extend and develop your experience as your imagination takes you on a journey of self-discovery and self-expression, and a moment of inspiration turns into a lifelong passion.

THE IMPACT OF THE DIGITAL AGE

There can be little doubt that our changing world has affected the way we communicate and document our lives, whether in the established areas of cinema and television, or through the new internet-based tools that offer a platform for our work which can be accessed by millions and transcends the borders of language and culture in a matter of seconds. There seems no limit, in fact, to where our creative energies can take us in the future and the possibilities we can explore, in a world that has become increasingly more informed and infinitely smaller, courtesy of technologies that have made our lives more instant, more compact and more accessible.

The advancement of audio visual technology

The digital age has not only transformed the way in which we make films but the way our work can be viewed, discussed, analysed and digested by the viewing audience and accessed through a choice of giant screens, conventional television sets, CD-ROM, DVD, computer hard drives or mobile telephones. The staggering advancement in audio visual technology has produced a mind-numbing array of lightweight, portable equipment that offers instant playback and can overcome almost any technical problems, leaving us free to express ourselves by whatever means we choose – that choice being enhanced as we review, manipulate and sculpture our rushes in one of the most creative environments of all, the digital edit suite, where programmes can be fashioned faster than ever before into personal mini-masterpieces.

The importance of creative integrity

But technology alone cannot produce powerful films that entertain audiences or take them on emotional roller-coaster journeys of discovery and revelation, for the ingredients needed to make such compelling works remain what they have always been – motivation, perspiration and craftsmanship. And these can only be achieved by perseverance and dedication, combined with a natural ability to tell a well-structured story that can penetrate our emotions, raise human consciousness and ask us to see the world in a different way, whilst having total respect for the audiences who rely on us to be honest and fair in our interpretation of events. No amount of technological artistic dressing can conceal the cracks in a badly conceived story that lacks direction, or focus, since the film-maker's creative integrity and sense of responsibility will always be embedded at the very core of the work he or she produces.

EXCITING NEW CHALLENGES FOR FILM-MAKERS

And the challenges are greater than ever, because our constantly evolving world has created extraordinary changes in the forces of nature, in the way we interact in a multicultural society, adapt to the global threat of terror and portray those less fortunate who are coping with severe hardship and illness. We need to try to capture all of this whilst trying to spread our resources across infinite multi-platform possibilities.

In broadcast television alone, hundreds of channels swallow up programme content faster than we could ever have dreamed possible. Although the future may herald a new age of video-on-demand and user-generated content, the current reality for the majority of film-makers who are passionate about creating thought-provoking and professional work, is that films need to be financed and commissioned if they are to reach a responsive audience who want to be truly stimulated. The mounting choice presented to the viewing public, however, means that ultimately they will decide *what* they want to watch, *when* they want to watch it, and just *how* they will watch it – possibly the greatest challenge to those producers, directors and commissioners whose opinions have dominated our viewing habits for so long.

OVERCOMING RESTRICTIONS AND PRESSURES

But whilst the growth in broadcast channels has created choice for viewers and producers alike, it has also placed increasing restrictions and pressure on film-makers, who have their budgets and schedules continually squeezed, to the point where directors find they have to supply more inventive product on increasingly less resources, which means less set-up time, less filming time, and less time to piece their rushes together coherently in the edit suite. Such are the pressures that professional film-makers live with on a daily basis, whether they work in documentary or drama, yet many produce work of great significance and value because they understand how to make the system work best for them, in tandem with a natural aptitude for the task in hand, accumulated experience and a disciplined approach. Being properly organised, in fact, is often the key to success and thorough preparation the greatest single investment that you will ever make on a film, whether that film lasts one minute or two hours, is a mini drama or a documentary.

Shooting economically

The need to shoot economically is paramount, especially on documentary shoots where events may take an unexpected turn, or the forces of nature turn dramatically against you. Having a game plan, giving yourself options and being organised can help you overcome seemingly insurmountable obstacles that threaten to wreck or severely hamper your project. In the following pages we will look at various ways in which you can adopt a number of working practices that will help you to achieve your objectives and keep you focused, so that you can produce a worthy and well-crafted film with the least amount of compromise, if any.

DECIDING WHAT KIND OF FILM-MAKER YOU WANT TO BE

Before getting involved in such detail, it would be wise for you to determine what kind of film-maker you want to be. You might simply want to make a short two-minute item for distribution on the internet, or opt for making short films to show what you are capable of, or for submission to broadcast television, the latter offering a multitude of channels and a wide audience, though here, for the most part, you are at the behest of the personal preferences of a commissioning editor or executive producer.

Using any short films you have made to enter into film festivals or send to producers in order to gain a foothold in the industry is certainly a worthwhile game plan, and although working as an employee for a film company or a broadcaster may mean making films that are formulaic or fit into an available transmission slot, the experience gained is ultimately worth the effort. There are few who can aspire to be Nick Broomfields, Barbara Kopples or Michael Moores at their first attempts, so spending some time learning the ropes is a way to avoid poverty and help you decide when the time is right to strike out and make your mark.

How to make your film stand out from the crowd

How to make sure you (and your films) stand out from the crowd is obviously something you need to think seriously about, because whatever your skills and talents, film-making is a highly competitive industry. As we work our way through this book we will look at some of the available options you might favour. Much depends, of course, on whether you see film as a pure art form, or as a commercial prospect that embraces creative expression. Choice again is relevant as you evaluate your options.

■ Will you take the more controlled, conventional route, or be totally spontaneous and reactionary – or will you employ a combination of styles and techniques, whether stylised, surreal or abstract, to tell your story?

- Will your film be purely observational, or will it be more subjective, constantly scratching beneath the sensory surface of the people you film?

- Will it keep to a chosen dramatic style, or cross the line between fiction and non-fiction?

- Will it tackle social issues, be provocative, entertaining, or take a humorous, satirical approach?

- Will it reflect to the viewer the known, or the unknown, or a combination of the two?

The short film revival

In considering these options, and many others we will look at later, it is clear that making a short film is not a simple matter of picking up a camera and creating an instant master work, so it's well worth taking the time to consider how you feel you can best express yourself and why it's important to explore the full range of possibilities. With such choice now available it's not surprising that in recent years there has been a small explosion of video diaries and mini dramas, mostly accessed on the internet. Documentary has enjoyed a significant revival, with many broadcasters, including the Discovery, Biography and History channels, embracing documentary almost exclusively, and the growth of short and documentary film festivals worldwide has given thousands of film-makers a global opportunity to showcase their work.

CONSIDERING YOUR AUDIENCE'S EXPECTATIONS

In analysing your role as a film-maker it is also worth remembering that just as the grammar of film has become more refined over the years, so have audience expectations. Pace in both filmed action and editing, greater variety of camera angles, jump-cuts (the intentional omission of action within shots to make them physically 'jump' position on screen) and transitions between scenes that allow the viewer to 'fill in' some of the gaps, are just a few of the techniques that audiences have now become familiar with and they offer a raft of new challenges to future generations of directors, editors and technicians.

Keeping your message clear

This is not to suggest that films should become overtly experimental or employ techniques which risk alienating the vast majority of their audience, since the viewer's basic need – to be informed with clarity, and entertained with a sense of fun – has changed little over the years, and although many of us want films that are thought-provoking and innovative, few of us would wish to sit in either an auditorium or our favourite armchair only to be blasted with meaningless imagery, an array of special effects, or be expected to understand the director's cleverly disguised and profound message by attending therapy sessions for several weeks afterwards. In most instances less is definitely more, and simplicity the key to success.

We will always, however, need film-makers who will challenge our conventions, our doctrines, our politics, our social ethics, the way we live and the way we die, and whatever the methods and whatever the chosen style, the medium of film and video will continue to offer an exciting range of possibilities and alternatives to all who take up the challenge.

2

The Film Legacy

It is hard to imagine how different our observations of life in, say, the late 1400s would be today if every household then had been in possession of a camcorder. Today we take for granted that we live in a world of instant playback; the sights and sounds before us captured in a tapestry of colour, vision and sound that is instantly accessible, providing future generations with startlingly realistic evidence of how we worked and played during our time on the planet.

THE ROLE OF FILM

Film has educated and entertained us for nearly 120 years and, although a relatively short timespan in the wider scheme of things, it has kept us informed through extraordinary periods of revolution and reform, helped us sustain our morale through two world wars, tackled changes in social attitudes and perceptions throughout the twentieth century and into the digital age of the twenty-first century, often working alongside governments, doctors, scientists, artists and experts of all kinds to enrich our lives beyond measure.

THE PIONEERING SPIRIT

A great many people are responsible for the creation and development of film in all its forms and although it is easy enough now for any of us to take to the streets with a camera and make a personal statement without recourse to history or to any of the established conventions, it is worth pausing to reflect that many of the early pioneers risked their reputations, their money, and sometimes their lives in order to make this extraordinary medium of expression readily available to us. *And we can learn much from their resourcefulness, since many of the ideas and techniques they founded are still practised throughout the world today and have become an established part of film grammar, despite the significant advances in technical innovation.*

Although no one person can be credited with the invention of the moving image, several jockey for position. Once the still photograph had become a part of our lives in the late nineteenth century, it was only a matter of time before the means was discovered to make such images flicker into life, courtesy of various dedicated innovators throughout America and Europe.

America gives us the Kinetoscope

Thomas Alva Edison, an American inventor of, among other things, the phonograph, built an early prototype of the motion picture camera, the Kinetoscope, in 1888 and copyrighted his first moving film, *The Sneeze*, featuring his assistant Fred Ott. By 1910, Edison had begun making a raft of entertainment and educational films, with early documentary-style projects depicting scenes of modern life which were edited to unify the films into a narrative whole.

France hosts the first public demonstration

In France, Auguste and Louis Lumière gave the first ever public film screening, showing ten observational shorts in Paris on 28

December 1895. It was also the first public demonstration of their Cinematograph. One film showed workers leaving factory gates, and another showed a train passing through a station, which had audiences diving for cover under their seats. *As we look more closely at the history of documentary, one recurring and fascinating aspect is just how audience reactions to the medium have changed over the years. When you consider how we are often amused at some of the cinematic conventions of the 40s, 50s, 60s and even 70s, it becomes easier to understand why audiences responded as they did to a speeding train back in 1895.*

Hidden treasures

Britain too had a part to play in the early development of film. Discovered only recently in the basement of a shop in Blackburn, England, are the works of Sagar Mitchell and James Kenyon. Now fully restored, this nitrate film forms part of an amazing collection made by Mitchell and Kenyon, one of the largest film producers in the UK at the end of the nineteenth century. Between 1900 and 1913, they showed observational films of workers leaving factories (obviously the popular genre of its day), promenading at the seaside, or engaged in various street and river activities. Many of the films were commissioned by local businesses, all screened at fairs by a network of showmen.

Novelty value and a lack of mobility

Because cameras were heavy and bulky and not terribly mobile, they were put into one position where they simply observed people walking past in silent but active procession. As film-makers became more ambitious these early cameras were mounted on various moving vehicles and were able to track, albeit slowly, among the bemused masses, creating an extra dimension to the scenes. Whilst the resulting films vividly documented the way people lived at the turn of the nineteenth century, they were still only regarded as having novelty and entertainment value, their true worth not yet being realised or exploited.

DOCUMENTARY COMES OF AGE

In 1922, the Russian film-maker Dziga Vertov established Kino-Pravda (film truth), one of the first recognised documentary movements, and a landmark in documentary film-making came in the same year when the American prospector and explorer Robert Flaherty made *Nanook of the North* as a direct result of living among the Inuit people in the Canadian arctic for several months.

Bending the truth

The original film was destroyed in a fire but Flaherty decided to return and start again, this time making the film more episodic and less like a travelogue. Unfortunately, this meant staging many of the scenes, including the Inuits using traditional harpoons for hunting instead of guns, and a family taking shelter from the elements in an igloo that had been sliced in half to let in the light and house the camera. Flaherty was determined to show man's fragile relationship with the harshest environmental conditions and although the film attracted criticism for its scenes of fictionalised reality, the story was an accurate depiction of life as the Inuits had traditionally lived it for hundreds of years.

The blurring of lines between dramatic reconstruction and reality is a convention that has been used extensively by documentary film-makers across the globe ever since and something we shall examine more closely later.

Flaherty establishes documentary conventions

Whatever methods Flaherty resorted to in order to make his film, he is unquestionably one of the founding fathers of the documentary form as we now know it, establishing the convention of living with a film's subjects as a participant-observer and becoming familiar with their way of life before attempting to film them, and structuring the narrative to engage the viewer and incorporate conflict at every opportunity. *Whilst today's film-makers might consider that moving in and living with their subjects for several weeks before filming might be taking dedication a bit far, the principle of getting to know your participants and gaining their trust is as relevant now as it ever was – and structuring a narrative is a device that can not only save time during shooting but give the film-maker a strong sense of focus throughout the production of a film.*

As far back as 1922 Flaherty was already experimenting with innovative ideas. He even employed two Akeley gyroscope cameras on *Nanook of the North* so that he could pan and tilt, even in extreme cold weather, and set up equipment to develop and print his footage on location so that he could review it in a makeshift theatre. Few would argue that such commitment and passion is the bedrock of the growth of documentary film as an important medium of communication.

The concept of film-making as a collaborative effort

Commissioned in 1929 to make *Drifters*, a ground-breaking film about the North Sea herring fleet, John Grierson went on to become a prolific producer and director, particularly influential through his creation of film units within the Empire Marketing

Board and the Post Office, thus nurturing a whole generation of documentary film-makers. In 1936, he produced the celebrated *Night Mail,* one of the first documentaries to use sound, with a script by WH Auden and music score by Benjamin Britten.

Grierson is credited with creating the term documentary, calling it 'the creative treatment of reality' and although his role as producer is well documented, his specific achievement as a director is not so easy to appraise, since the documentary movement he founded took a collaborative approach to production. Whilst Grierson is only credited with directing *Drifters,* he encouraged the various talent of young film-makers such as Basil Wright and Humphrey Jennings and influenced entire generations who followed in his wake.

PROPAGANDA AND THE WAR YEARS

Between 1939 and 1945, as the Second World War grew in intensity and the political and tactical ramifications resounded across the globe, film-makers on every continent quickly came to realise that film could be employed in the war effort as a mighty propaganda tool. Some, like Adolf Hitler, had been rousing the German nation long before war broke out in a staggering succession of films designed to get the nation back to work whilst enthusing them about building a New Germany after the collapse of the country's economy following the First World War.

The power of film

What most of the German nation did not realise was that Hitler had his own agenda. Such is the power of film that the Third Reich used it extensively in pursuit of its own political ideals, not least of which was a little matter of world domination and the creation of an Arian super race.

Masterminding this cavalcade of spin was a former dancer and actress, Leni Riefenstahl, who had been making exceptionally polished and artistic movies, which set realistic stories in fairyland mountain settings, before being asked by Hitler to bring her poetic vision to his cause. When it came to showing blonde, blue-eyed men running around in corn fields, or curvy maidens tossing balls to each other with gay abandon on sandy beaches to reinforce the message 'enjoy a better future with the Third Reich', Riefenstahl was in her element. And when Hitler opened massive armament factories to build tanks and aircraft that were displayed at mass rallies in Berlin, accompanied by thousands of banners, marching soldiers and rousing brass band or choral music, Riefenstahl was on hand to make sure it was all given maximum creative and political impact.

FILM AND THE ART OF DECEPTION

Although many of Hitler's generals felt they were not yet ready for war, the Führer over-ruled them. He knew he had built up a frightening image of a country ready to crush its enemies and with such powerful propaganda films as *Triumph of the Will* exploiting the new might of Germany, news soon spread that Hitler was not someone to mess with.

Despite mounting criticism of Riefenstahl's association with the Nazi Party, she continued to make documentaries after the war up to her death in 2003 at the age of 101, even surviving a helicopter crash at the age of 98 whilst filming in the Sudan. Putting aside the dubious and deceptive messages behind her Nazi war films,

Leni Riefenstahl proved herself to be a tenacious and formidable film-maker.

A trick of the light

Germany, however, wasn't alone in creating an illusion to distort the reality. The British government, in tandem with many others throughout the world, was producing a whole range of films designed to keep the nation's spirits high and to boost morale. Workers were no longer seen wandering from factory gates as in Mitchell and Kenyon's day; they were actively working their socks off for the war effort inside the factories, singing their hearts out to melodies on the radio, whilst others were being recruited into the armed forces in readiness for the coming fight. The true horrors of what was happening across Europe were hidden as much as possible behind this façade of endeavour, since the grim realities of war were not the most inspirational and motivational images to put before hardworking, well-meaning citizens who just wanted to be rid of their enemies and get on with their lives.

And if you were to ever wonder how millions of people's minds can be manipulated so easily, you need look no further than the role film and video can play in political spin, advertising and the cult of celebrity adulation today. Cleverly devised moving images and their sound tracks can be highly influential in the hands of those who know how to use them to maximum effect. In the following pages we will explore the various ways that information can be relayed at a conscious and sub-conscious level, and the responsibility we have as film-makers to use our integrity in order to get to the truth without misleading and deceiving either our audience or the people we film.

NEW INNOVATIONS IN THE POST-WAR YEARS

When the war was over, everyone's focus was on picking up the pieces and generating social stability. Things could never be the same but there was real hope that a better future could be created from the physical and emotional rubble, and film played a vital role in uniting everyone to the cause.

Film as an inspirational force

Governments commissioned hundreds of documentaries and short films to illustrate just what was being done – and what needed to be done – to get their countries back on their feet. In the aftermath of the war, television was not set to truly come of age worldwide until the early 1950s – marked in Britain by the Coronation of Queen Elizabeth II in 1953 – so cinema remained the most influential means of communication. Series such as Britain's *Look at Life* were screened between the main features to show a somewhat sanitised view of our lives, with jolly music and patronising commentary designed to help us look forward to the future with optimism and hope.

A new generation of film-makers emerges

By the end of the 1950s a new and enterprising group of film-makers began to make their mark and take advantage of the new cameras that offered much greater flexibility and portability than had been possible before, incorporating synch sound recording during shoots, even in the most seemingly inaccessible of places.

Cinéma-vérité – cinema of truth – a technique of using hand-held cameras to become active participants in people's lives and capturing events at their most natural, was the benchmark of

French film-makers such as Jean Rouch. Also known as Direct Cinema, the form has been used extensively by such luminaries as Michel Brault, Barbara Kopple, the Maysles brothers, Richard Leacock and Robert Drew. *Primary,* for example, followed candidates John F Kennedy and Hubert Humphrey as they walked among the crowds and held meetings in hotel rooms during the 1960 primary election in the United States, with greater intimacy than had ever been seen before. DA Pennebaker focused on direct and uninterrupted observation in films such as *Don't Look Back,* featuring Bob Dylan, whilst one of his contemporaries, Fred Wiseman, observed human conversation and the routines of everyday life without music or narration, in films like *Law and Order, Hospital* and *Welfare.*

Cinéma-vérité has, however, attracted some criticism over the years, because it is argued that you cannot be an unobtrusive and objective observer attempting to obtain a true picture of reality if your very presence influences how people react when on camera (an important debate that we shall discuss in more detail as we work our way through later chapters). Despite such reservations, this form of natural filming is still used in documentary today and is a technique employed by certain cinema directors, for example Francois Truffaut, Jean Luc Goddard and Paul Greengrass in films such as The Bourne Ultimatum, *and television series such as* The State Within, *to give fictional stories a greater sense of realism.*

Whatever your viewpoint, the late 1950s and early 60s created a wave of new thinking, which is an influential factor in defining our own roles as film-makers today.

THE EVOLUTION OF THE FICTIONAL FILM

Early feature films did not associate themselves so much with the realities of life, since nobody had any particular desire to leave their problems at home only to be confronted by them again on a giant screen. Silent films concentrated almost exclusively on entertaining the masses, and comedy in particular was high on the cinematic agenda, thanks to the likes of Chaplin, Keaton and Laurel and Hardy.

Devoid of sound, other than the occasional piano accompaniment, silent films of the early 1900s drew audiences into their story by inviting them to use their own imaginations in supplying the voices and the sound effects, thus enhancing the experience.

The learning curve

Studying films from the silent era up to the mid-1940s shows just how much advancement we have made in the techniques of fictional story-telling. Lingering theatrical wide shots; over-emphasis of dramatic expression; lighting with heavy shadows to give dramatic impetus; make-up and wardrobe to differentiate between good and evil – all gradually replaced by closer, more revealing shots; subtle, minimal acting; make-up, wardrobe and lighting that blends in naturally with the characters and their surroundings.

No longer do actors have to theatrically throw their hands to their foreheads to illustrate emotional turmoil, or cowboys wear white hats and black hats to tell us who we should be rooting for in a gunfight – but it is worth bearing in mind that no such conventions seemed strange or comical to audiences at the time. The growing sophistication of audiences has led us to be much more flexible with the fictional film form today, with films such as *Memento* telling a complete narrative in reverse, or *Groundhog Day* repeating scenes over and over, dropping vast chunks of narrative each time as the audience 'jumps' the gap from one part of the story to the next.

Film-makers such as Edwin S Porter had pioneered the concept of cross-cutting in the 1903 film *The Great Train Robbery* to show simultaneous action in different places, and Sergei Eisenstein introduced the concept of 'montage', the juxtaposition of images for vivid dramatic effect, in films such as *Battleship Potemkin* in 1925. Yet feature films that were made some 20 years later were still cutting in on the same line, from wide shot to close shot, without any noticeable change of angle and causing a continuity jump, and there was little that was particularly exciting or innovative in cinema for several years.

Sound adds a new dimension

Although many film-makers claimed their film to be the first with a soundtrack, the 1926 cinema release *Don Juan* was the first feature to use a completely synchronised soundtrack, with the Vitaphone system, followed in 1927 by *The Jazz Singer*, the first 'talking' picture, which effectively sounded the death knell for silent films and ushered in a new era of fictional film-making.

3

Deciding on an Approach

Whatever length of film you plan to make, be it two minutes or ten, your prime objective is to make your story as interesting and compelling as possible. Stimulating your audience can be achieved in numerous ways, but you first need to make some decisions on your filmic style, which may utilise any number of possibilities:

- *documentary, documentary-drama, or drama*
- *objective or subjective*
- *real or surreal*
- *conventional or abstract*
- *artistic or commercial*
- *specialist or of universal appeal.*

ASSESSING THE OPTIONS

When cinéma-vérité swept into the arena in the late 1950s many respected film directors began using this technique of fly-on-the-wall observational filming because of the mobility it allowed and the access it gave. Some documentary film-makers, like Jennifer Fox, became concerned that this approach was not completely objective, because the presence of the film-maker actually conditions events, and watching action does not reveal a great deal if you don't know what the subject is thinking or feeling. For her, interviewing people penetrates their psychology and motivation, which in turn reveals a fuller depth of character.

Cinéma-vérité in documentary does, of course, allow the subject matter to breathe, often uncluttered by voice tracks, narration and even music, relying solely on natural sounds to tell the story. The downside is that although this technique does employ a style which can, at best, be very effective, watching this kind of film for more than a few minutes risks inducing frustration and impatience in the viewer as new levels of information and stimulation are often needed to hold their interest.

CREATIVITY AND THE TRUTH

Likewise, you need to seriously consider whether your film will reflect the absolute truth of a given situation or a *version* of the truth. The Canadian film-maker William Greaves observes that it is the creative input that signals the value of a film-maker, so if you just put your camera down and simply record the sights and sounds before you, how does that, on its own, raise human consciousness?

For his 1959 film *Emergency Ward*, Greaves recorded a soundtrack of a patient screaming at a nurse, but was unable to shoot any pictures. He filmed a nurse later interacting with an unseen patient in silhouette against a curtain and ran the pre-recorded soundtrack to it, giving the impression that both were happening simultaneously. Purists might argue that the staging of a scene in this way is a distortion of the truth, yet there was nothing fabricated within the soundtrack, which accurately reflected the confrontation. The visuals simply gave a stylistic interpretation of the incident – the creative input that Greaves feels is often necessary, and important, in defining the film-maker's role.

The skill of creative interpretation

For film-makers like William Greaves, adopting the technique of vérité filming is one thing, but not to the exclusion of artistic expression or creative input. Bill could have added that it's a heck of lot more fun to take a bunch of rushes, mix them up, move the voice tracks around and add some music, thus increasing the enjoyment level for both the film-maker and the audience. Which does not mean you need, or should, in any way distort the overall objective of the film or the truth within it. The depiction of truth, or a creative version of it, is something that may affect how you approach your film so it is worth taking a look at some of the options.

Dramatic interpretation

For many films, particularly those that make reference to past events, dramatic reconstruction may be the only effective way of illustrating your story, used in the absence of, or in conjunction with, photographs, newspaper cuttings, drawings, old letters, maps and graphics. If your short film is a documentary that requires drama sequences you will need to factor in any combination of:

- script
- rehearsals
- auditions
- wardrobe
- make-up
- props
- set design.

If your film is a historical drama-documentary you should obviously ensure it is historically accurate in terms of dialogue, wardrobe and props and be aware of the problems involved in creating a world that no longer exists. Some films may require a dramatic reconstruction that has relevance to the present day – a crime reconstruction for example, or an eye witness account of a particular incident. The BBC series *999* featured stories of ordinary people caught up in emergency situations, effectively combining interviews and voice tracks with dramatic reconstruction. This kind of film often employs two very different filming styles – the controlled tripod-on-camera method for filming the interviewees and a hand-held, all-action approach that makes a dynamic contrast between the two. In some instances you may even decide to give the action scenes a distinct visual look in order to inject more stylisation into the film and make the contrast between the two techniques even more pronounced.

A difference of approach

If you are making a drama or a documentary short which will include drama reconstructions, however, your filming approach will generally be quite different from documentary, taking into account:

- dramatic angle changes between shots
- overlapping of action to create the most effective edit points
- continuity of action
- awareness of eyelines
- matching of sound between set-ups.

Artistic licence

Going a step further, you may feel it appropriate to create a surreal or abstract look to your film. There is a distinction, however, between art for art's sake and a stylised approach, particularly in documentary film-making. Art may be fun, but will not disguise a badly constructed story. Integrating stylisation into a strong narrative, however, can be extremely effective. A meaningful examination of a person's nightmares or recurring dreams, for example, may help us understand the seriousness of the person's problem with the use of some carefully constructed abstract scenes. Whilst it can be argued that such scenes give only an impression of 'the truth', it could also be argued that they are not distorting the subject's real-life experiences if spoken with sincerity and even a sense of fear. A visual interpretation of a situation is, for me, perfectly acceptable if the spine of the story reflects the subjects' experiences with honesty and integrity. It could also provide another level of information whilst heightening the viewers' own emotional responses.

BLURRING THE LINES

There is a marked difference, however, in making your filmic conventions clear to an audience, and creating a false or misleading interpretation of people and events. When we watch a work of fiction we know that everything is a figment of someone's imagination or the director's visualisation of a story, whether that story be original or a fictionalised account of an actual event. With factual, documentary and documentary-drama films the lines are not always as clearly drawn and it is very easy to give an interpretation of the truth, or even distort the truth, either by accident or by design.

Real or imaginary

In 1965, Peter Watkins followed the success of his BBC drama-documentary *Culloden,* about the Jacobite uprising of 1745–6, with a startling vision of Britain under nuclear attack. *The War Game* was deemed so frighteningly realistic by the authorities that it was banned from being broadcast for over 20 years, when it was finally decided that audiences would no longer be so traumatised by the experience that they would throw themselves behind their armchairs in terrified droves. *The War Game*, although listed in Channel 4's compilation of all-time top documentaries, is not a documentary but a work of fiction made in documentary style so that it appears more earthy and believable. To that end it was highly effective and won a clutch of awards.

By coincidence, Gillo Pontecorvo's film *The Battle of Algiers*, made in the same year, fictionally recreates, with a distinct newsreel look, the years preceding the 1962 Algerian revolution. It is so chillingly authentic that although it has been banned in both the USA and France over the years, military personnel at the Pentagon have used it as a field guide to fighting terrorism. Using a cast of amateur actors, many of whom had fought in the actual battles represented in the film, *The Battle of Algiers* is often cited as an example of incendiary, documentary-style political film-making at its best.

Film realism and its influence on society

In the 1966 film *Cathy Come Home* writer Jeremy Sandford shows in stark detail an ordinary family's decline into poverty and homelessness. The director Ken Loach adopted a gritty documentary style in telling the story of a young couple starting married life full of hope and optimism but becoming scarred by misfortune, separation and eviction, and culminating in one of television's most unforgettable scenes as Cathy's two children are taken away from her, in a state of hysteria, by Social Services. The scene was so realistic, in fact, that many viewers must have believed that it was being played for real.

Cathy Come Home illustrates the enormous influence that film can have on society – tremendous outrage following its broadcast about the state of housing in Britain and the role of the authorities, who appeared uncaring and hostile – and giving rise to a feeling of bias in its representation of a real life situation. The film, however, is a landmark in drama and established powerful new conventions, contributing substantially to the public and political debates that followed.

THE DIRECTOR'S VISION

In 1966, two schoolboys, Kevin Brownlow and Andrew Mollo, made a monumental re-enactment of what might have happened if the Nazis had invaded Britain. After eight years of problems and obstacles, they completed their epic film, *It Happened Here*, with hundreds of volunteers and thousands of authentic historical props and uniforms. The scenes are so realistic that anyone could be forgiven for thinking that the majority of the film was compiled from archive footage taken in 1945 and not reconstructed in 1966.

These film-makers did not set out to fool their audience. They simply wanted to give us their vision of the future had the unthinkable happened, and to create awareness of the consequences if it ever did. To achieve this objective the imagery had to be as gritty and convincing as possible and the approach taken was to film *It Happened Here* as a drama in documentary style. Brownlow and Mollo are tremendous examples to all aspiring film-makers; their tenacity in completing a film against all the odds an extraordinary accomplishment that has since achieved legendary status in cinema history.

Film-making from the heart

Above everything, film-making should always be an exhilarating and rewarding experience, whether you are making a snappy, fun-packed comic short, or a lyrical poetic retrospective, or tackling a piece of in-depth investigative journalism. Films do not always have to have a hidden message or prick our conscience or reflect the problems of society. They can also be an expression of our imagination in its raw, top-of-the-head state – and why not? You *should* make films about the things that inspire you; that make people laugh or cry; about subjects you feel strongly about, or that many of us are blissfully ignorant of, or just on a creative whim.

D A Pennebaker's 1956 film short, *Daybreak Express*, is a kaleidoscope of music and imagery of a day in the life of New York seen from a moving train packed with people. It is observational in style, devoid of any real detail about the town or its people, yet despite its flashing imagery of skyscrapers and speeding slabs of grimy metal, evokes a strange natural beauty.

The National Film and Television School film *The Score*, made some 50 years later, shows a day in the life of thousands of football fans making their way to a match; a carnival of colourful sights and sounds that gives a snapshot of British life without making any specific comment on why these supporters are so fixated by the sport.

Both films could have been turned from objective to subjective simply by adding a layer of voices of the people involved to give us a deeper insight into their thoughts and feelings, but this was not the approach the film-makers' intended to take. For them, observation was not only a part of their chosen filming style but a personal creative statement.

HAVING FUN WITH YOUR FILM

Humour is a subject chosen by many as a first film and the techniques employed to give universal enjoyment to audiences are many and varied. Richard Penfold and Sam Hearn's excellent four-minute film *Dog Years* shows a castrated mongrel running about on a beach with his owner as he tells us, in voice-over, how he has adapted to life without any testicles. The film was shot on Super 8mm on a single 150ft roll and edited in camera, giving it a unique, lyrical, almost surreal quality.

Alex Ryan's 2004 comic caper *Fester! Fester!* features two lads being pushed at high speed in a couple of shopping trolleys by two mates intent on reaching the finishing line before the other. The contest is covered with the same filmic energy as a Formula One race, the edits having identical dynamics as we cut from side angles, to high angles, from low angles to tracking shots, reinforced by a soundtrack of racing cars revving and screeching their way around a race track.

Imagination is everything

There is nothing particularly deep or profound in either of these films, but they are absorbing, and great fun, and show just how film-makers can use their imaginations to tell a simple story on limited resources.

And even when film-makers have something pertinent and meaningful to say, innovative simplicity can create a richly textured experience.

Dan Wilson's student film *Square Eyes* captures a day in the life of a couch potato seen through the 'eye' of his television set. Filmed on one locked-off shot and capturing a series of surrealistic imagery set to a bizarre music track, *Square Eyes* is an imaginative, abstract, modern fable which culminates in the main character being abducted from his living room and dumped into a TV hell of his own.

By contrast, *Queen of Stone*, a film by Martin Christian, uses one continuous hand-held shot to illustrate a child attempting to escape her feuding, self-absorbed parents through her own imagination. The film is beautiful and evocative, with no dialogue, and relies solely on engaging imagery and an abstract visual narrative to tell a poignant story. Ben Dodd's *Surprise* is another short film taken on one continuous shot, only this dramatic one-minute gem tells its story in reverse.

Such inspirational films, from emerging directors with little or no previous experience, prove that the future for the creative mediums are as bright as ever.

4

A New Box of Tricks

From the late 1950s cinema audiences began to slowly dwindle as television became the new, must-have accessory in everyone's home. Factories throughout Europe had already been turned over to making such consumer desirables as refrigerators, radios and washing machines to meet the demands of nations rebuilding their lives and intent on creating a more comfortable and practical home environment. The social and political landscape was about to change dramatically as people began to demand better and more exciting lifestyles. A new wave of writers bombarded the stage with 'new realism' plays criticising the Establishment, not only transforming the theatre overnight but sowing the seeds for television to pick up the baton in the following years with cutting satire, 'kitchen sink' dramas, and socially conscious documentaries.

TELEVISION CREATES A WIDER AUDIENCE

Whilst the early days of television brought us a plethora of studio-bound do-it-yourself shows and cookery programmes, fresh and interesting formats soon began to emerge, which in turn established new conventions and ideas from which many present day formats have been developed. Drama, which up to then had been universally accepted as 90 minutes of escapist entertainment you sat and watched on a large screen in a theatre, became a mix of entertainment and gritty realism on a small screen in your living room and running at various lengths from half an hour to two hours – heralding, among other things, the arrival of the soap opera.

Documentary and factual programmes were ushered in on a tidal wave of enterprise, covering a vast range of subject matter, of varying lengths, to stimulate our interest and open our eyes to what was happening in the world, with much more immediacy than cinema had been able to provide. The BBC purchased Ealing Film Studios in 1955 – the studio's feature film-making activities now on the wane – and set about making dramas and documentaries with fervour.

Innovation and individual style

One influential film-maker who came to the fore during this period was the *enfant terrible* of cinema, Ken Russell. Russell achieved fame and notoriety with cinema films such as *Savage Messiah* and *The Devils*, but prior to this had cut his teeth making documentaries for the BBC's *Monitor* and *Omnibus* series, having aroused interest with his earlier work as a short film-maker. Early amateur films such as *Amelia and the Angel*, made in 1958, are classic examples of how to make a short film on a virtually non-existent budget.

Made as a statement to Russell's new found faith in Catholicism, the film features a nine-year-old girl who is rehearsing the part of an angel for a school play, but cannot resist taking the wings home to show her mother. Her brother steals the wings and damages them beyond repair, leaving a guilt-ridden Amelia to try to find redemption and a new pair of wings before the play is performed. There is no synchronised sound, the entire soundtrack consists of library music and snatches of narration, and many of the tracking shots were filmed from an old pram. Yet the film is full of striking visual interpretations that combine fantasy with reality. It is a superb example of what can be accomplished without adequate resources and relying almost totally on the director's unique vision and surrealistic filming style.

In the two years I spent at Ealing Studios in the mid-60s, Russell made his iconic films about Isadora Duncan and Elgar, and the BBC Adventure Unit set out regularly on journeys of discovery, searching for some lost tribe of cannibals up the Amazon or wherever, gone for weeks and months on end – with no satellite links or mobile phones to help keep contact – until they turned up at the studio gates with piles of film cans that were waiting to be processed so that millions of viewers could relive the excitement and dangers of the expedition.

Discovering new ideas

These early television film-makers pioneered many techniques that have become a part of documentary grammar as well as the short film form, including the deployment of portable equipment, with sound, to some of the most remote and hazardous terrain on the planet. Monsoons, raging rapids, hostile natives, unfamiliar and treacherous jungles, all conspired to challenge the film-makers as they worked to structure gripping stories under extremes of pressure and unpredictability.

But filming lost tribes in forgotten corners of the world was only one of many avenues of exploration that television was starting to embrace and fashion into new and inventive genres, including:

- exploration and discovery
- natural history

- historical retrospectives
- drama series
- investigative documentary
- personality-led films
- expert-led films
- home improvement programmes
- makeover programmes
- reality television.

All of these programme genres are still with us today and, in a new climate of opportunity, television has recognised that there is also a place for short films and created specialist transmission slots to accommodate them, with the likes of 'Three Minute Wonder' and 'FourDocs'.

A wide range of programme genres

In 1995, BBC Bristol commissioned a short film *Talking Trees,* a portrayal of men and women in Northern Ireland who have a passion for trees. It reinforces the point that films of this kind do not always have to fall into any specific pigeon holes of objectivity, subjectivity or fly-on-the-wall immediacy. They can also be lyrical and stylish, yet informative and emotive as they employ beautiful imagery, carefully crafted shot composition, dynamic angle changes and gentle tracking shots to tell their story and make their point.

Television, then, offers an amazing range of programming genres to satisfy most of our needs, both as viewers and film-makers, and certainly has the potential to offer us a diverse choice of vibrant, quality programmes to keep us entertained and informed about our own communities and the wider world.

THE CHALLENGE TO BE INNOVATIVE

Not all of broadcasting's output, however, has been greeted with rapturous enthusiasm. Many question if much of television's output today continues to be fresh and stimulating and pointedly ask if so-called Reality Television, for example, is truly 'real' or counterfeit? Does it reflect people's lives with honesty and integrity, or is it stage-managed and manipulative, exploiting its participants and misleading its audience? Some reality formats of late have even begun to stage constructed scenarios in which ordinary people act out events as if they *are* for real. One might also reflect if sometimes the over-used convention of relentless, wall-to-wall voice narration to take us through an unfolding story fuels a lack of belief in the film-maker's ability to tell us the absolute truth rather than a constructed version of it – or our own ability to understand what is going on if the story arc is not made absolutely clear, step by step.

The blurring of the lines is still as much a subject for debate and serious consideration as it ever was. Our television diet today may consist of one successful format being cloned by another and the public's obsession with celebrity given maximum media coverage at every opportunity, but there is much to be thankful for. The need to be innovative will always be a part of the film-makers' psyche. Creative and forward-thinking individuals have always managed to somehow rise to the challenge and we can learn much from their achievements.

A roll-call of talent

In 1961, John Schlesinger gave us *Terminus* – an observational film of a day in the life of Waterloo Station and a fore-runner to such programmes as *Airport*. Paul Watson's 1974 documentary *The Family* was a pioneering fly-on-the-wall examination of the real life struggles of a working-class family from Reading, whilst Michael Apted's *Seven Up* followed a group of children in seven-year cycles as their perceptions of the world around them changed and they matured into adults asking penetrating questions about their changing circumstances and roles in society. *Grand Designs* and *No Going Back*, both outstanding series from Channel 4, show true human endeavour and perseverance in the face of adversity.

The BBC's *Walking with Dinosaurs* gives us an amazing insight into a world we would never have believed existed and David Attenborough's numerous forays into the natural world leave us breathless and much better informed about the wildlife we all too often take for granted.

Kenneth Clark, Robert Winston, Ray Mears and others share the honours as informed people who guide us through areas of life and history that might otherwise have passed us by. Louis Theroux continues to give us a master class in encouraging people from all walks of life to talk about themselves in a way that few of us could ever hope to accomplish – picking up the baton from Robert Flaherty and moving in with many of his subjects in order to gain a greater understanding of what makes them tick.

Devices and trickery

The BBC Adventure Unit may have long since ceased to exist, but exploration and discovery continues to feed our desire for the exotic and the mysterious, from Alan Whicker's journeys around the world to examine human beings' cultural differences, to Michael Palin's race against time in *Around the World in 80 Days*, which combined adventure with good humour, and a narrative drive shared by a personable presenter and several large slices of dramatic intrigue. Cliff-hangers at the end of each episode whetted our appetite for next week's adventure – a sleight-of-hand employed by film and programme-makers from the earliest B movies to the present day. Many short films and documentaries open with a teaser using sections extracted from somewhere in the middle of the film and placed up the front as a hook – a device that many editors and directors, including myself, have exploited to good effect over the years.

Whether we like it or not, we live in an age of instant gratification, and audiences can be extremely unforgiving if we are unable to tap quickly into their impulses and preferences. As we have discovered, however, those same audiences can be subconsciously led in a direction of our choosing if we know the right buttons to press in the structuring of our narrative.

LEADING BY EXAMPLE

Many film practitioners have been recognised for the individual contributions they have made to the craft, some by design, and others without seeking any particular recognition, but almost always by virtue of their imagination, dedication and resourcefulness.

Shooting from the hip

In 1970, Chris Bonington led an expedition up the south face of Annapurna for a Thames Television documentary series *The Hardest Way Up*. Amongst the team was mountaineer Mick Burke, who also happened to have a passion for photography. Armed with pickaxes, crampons and a film camera, Mick spent his days swinging perilously from crevasses and ice-caps, working his way up the mountainside in various extremes of weather and physical encumbrance whilst filming the ascent with meticulous care. His extraordinary footage, coupled with the professionally shot material, gave a vivid insight into the dangers and loneliness experienced by mountaineers. Some months after completing the film, Mick joined a team climbing Everest, again with a film camera as an essential part of his kit, but he fell to his death just a few weeks into the climb. Given a choice of how to exit when his number was called, Mick may not have wanted it any other way, but one thing is for sure – he would have been extremely chuffed to be thought of now as one of the film industry's first self-shooters.

Being aware of a film's visual flow

On the flip side, Claudio von Planta is a professional cameraman who seems to enjoy taking his life in his hands at every opportunity on filming expeditions. He is a supreme example to all film-makers of how to take shots that will edit into a compelling and dramatic narrative, without any direction and under extremes of pressure.

When Ewan McGregor and Charley Boorman decided to ride two motorbikes across Europe and the treacherous terrain of Russia, China and Alaska, en route to New York, they wisely abandoned the idea of filming the trip themselves and enlisted the help of Claudio to film the journey. Although he failed his motorcycle test just a few days before departure and the production team had to wait for him to catch up, Claudio's film diary of the journey is an extraordinary accomplishment.

Long Way Round grips you from beginning to end and never lets go. Its filming style is energetic and breathless and you live every moment of McGregor and Boorman's torments and joys. Even more remarkably, every scene is a testament to the natural instincts and understanding of film grammar by its cameraman. When McGregor's bike wheels spin in a sea of mud, Claudio not only puts his camera down to help push him out to safety, but makes sure the camera is recording the event even though he is not looking through the eyepiece. And when the motorcyclists come across a fast-flowing river that is clearly inaccessible and some locals are employed to drive a lorry through it with supplies, Claudio films a series of shots that would do any editor proud. There is not one scene in the entire ten-part series that does not ebb and flow thanks to the quality of the editing and the man who filmed the unfolding events.

Ewan McGregor and Charley Boorman can be justifiably pleased with the end result, but I am sure they are both very relieved to have taken a cameraman of the calibre of Claudio von Planta along for the ride.

All aspiring directors should try to perfect the knack of visualising a completed scene whilst on a shoot, or even better, on the recce. Running a scene in your head will not only show the shots you need, but the basic rhythm and tempo of the sequence. When Claudio filmed the river scene he visualized a combination of action shots of the lorry, the river, and cutaways of tense faces that he knew would edit into a fast-paced and highly effective scenario.

Observers or intruders

Nick Broomfield, who followed up his 1971 BFI-funded black-and-white film short *Who Cares*, with a documentary, *Proud to be British*, which he made as a student at the National Film and Television School, has earned a reputation in the field of documentary that is now legion. His participatory approach in door-stepping subjects and filming their reactions with a minimum crew – including himself in vision – is widely recognised as being distinctive if often disturbing. Some observers have labelled his style as 'performative' because his intrusion into a scene inevitably affects and alters the situation, but Nick Broomfield certainly gets people's attention and as viewers we are undoubtedly the beneficiaries, whatever the arguments about the truth only emerging from his provocative encounters with the film's subjects. When filming people who are quite deft at ducking awkward questions, or not willing to reveal very much about themselves or their dubious intentions, it often becomes necessary to rattle their cages a little in order to get at the truth.

One could hardly accuse Broomfield of being openly hostile or threatening, however, and aspiring film-makers would certainly benefit from studying films such as *Aileen* or *The Leader, His Driver and The Driver's Wife* to see how he elicits information by putting people on the spot in an often good-humoured and generally non-inflammatory manner. It should be remembered that Nick Broomfield, like Michael Moore, targets people who have put themselves in the firing line. Later we shall discuss the various approaches necessary when dealing with ordinary people who trust you to represent their views in a fair, honest and balanced way. Snapping relentlessly at people's heels is one thing – gaining their trust and co-operation quite another.

INTEGRATING STYLISATION INTO YOUR NARRATIVE

A superb example of combining style with uplifting and emotionally charged storytelling is Patrick Collerton's outstanding 2004 documentary *The Boy Whose Skin Fell Off*, about 36-year old Jonny Kennedy, who had a terrible genetic condition called Dystrophic Epidermolysis Bullosa. This meant that his skin literally came away from his body at the slightest contact. He was covered in agonising sores, resulting in a final fight against skin cancer, which eventually claimed him.

The Boy Whose Skin Fell Off could have been a conventional, chronological account of the life and ultimate death of a man tormented by continual pain. What separates this film from other explorations of human beings and their battle to overcome adversity is the innovative style in which it was made. The film opens with Jonny Kennedy lying slumped in a chair – dead – his voice-over informing us that he has come back in spirit to tell us about his life and his death.

The opening minute of this film is not only terribly poignant; it hooks the viewer immediately with its cheeky and audacious approach. Clearly, Patrick Collerton and Jonny Kennedy had made a conscious decision that the film would be a personal, imaginative, even surreal, journey, full of good humour, and sprinkled with surprises. As the film unfolds we get to know Jonny and realise that his collaboration with Collerton comes to us by way of a generosity of spirit and pure mischief-making, both essential parts of Kennedy's character.

In a later chapter we shall discuss the merits of constructing a creative template to work from before you go out filming. In other words, if you decide on a stylised approach, there are certain elements you need to factor into both your narrative and your filming schedule long before you arrive at your first location. In some scenes in The Boy Whose Skin Fell Off *Jonny Kennedy is seen flying in a glider, high among the clouds. It is no coincidence that Patrick Collerton is able to make an analogy in his final edit between the cavalier, fun-loving attitude of his subject as he drifts among the clouds, and the ethereal associations.*

Jonny Kennedy's final voice track, recorded as if he is sitting on a heavenly cloud to the accompaniment of Queen's 'Don't Stop Me Now', is heart-rending to say the least, and all the more powerful because of a narrative driven by both its subject and the film's ground-breaking style.

The need to innovate and inspire

Every so often, such masterpieces come along to make us sit up and take notice. Although many believe that television has been treading water for a while, broadcasters and commissioners with vision and courage often do take risks. Their investment in the many hundreds of people with individual talent and enterprising ideas will eventually pay dividends as we, the viewers, will be able to experience fresh, invigorating films made by those who have the ability to excite, motivate and enthuse.

5

Evaluating Your Options

In Chapter 1 we looked at just a few of the many options available to the film-maker, but there is no photo kit formula since a film is generally a creative expression brought to fruition by one person's vision. Many professional practitioners, in fact, will have their own personal – and very different – views on how to approach the making of any genre of film. I simply put the various options before you to consider and evaluate. Most importantly, you must first decide what kind of film you want to make.

- *Will your film be purely observational or subjective?*
- *What will drive the narrative?*
- *Will we understand where people stand within conflicts?*
- *Will the characters get what they want or need?*
- *Will the characters gain audience empathy?*
- *Will your film be informative, humorous, satirical, investigative?*
- *Will you employ a combination of styles and techniques?*
- *Can you use counterpoint?*
- *Will your film be textured or multi-layered?*
- *Can you hook your audience from the opening scene?*
- *Will it be artistic, commercial, or a combination of the two?*
- *Will it cross the line between non-fiction and fiction?*
- *Will your film be balanced and impartial or completely subjective?*

■ *Will your story be fully rounded or leave questions unanswered?*

■ *Will the film be slow and measured or pacy and dynamic?*

■ *Will your story have one or more defined turning points?*

■ *Can you disguise exposition?*

■ *Will you employ subtext within the narrative?*

■ *Will your film be compelling?*

The last of these options is, without question, the most important, because without an audience having the desire to watch your film the other possibilities in this list have little relevance. Your film does not need to have all *of these ingredients, just those that will combine to make the strongest narrative possible to tell your particular story.*

FINDING A STYLE

The examples of observational and subjective filming that we have looked at in previous chapters should help you focus on the basic style of your film, even if the content does not, on first consideration, give a clear indication of which route you should take. Following a rock band on a European tour, for instance, may seem to work best chronologically and in observational style, dynamically cutting between energetic stage performances, to exhausted bodies slumped inside a minibus driving through a rain-drenched night, windscreen wipers squeaking backwards and forwards, to riggers working frantically to get the next venue up and running before the punters arrive. This type of spontaneous approach, using vividly contrasting pictures with dramatic sound edits to tell the unfolding saga, might well work best – particularly if your subjects are not always approachable or able to express themselves articulately. Why litter the soundtrack, you might ask, with irrelevant, incoherent voices that add nothing to the story and might risk lessening its impact as a forceful, creative piece of film-making?

Consider the alternatives

On the other hand, if the members of the band are particularly outspoken and you feel they have something to say – and worth listening to – about music, travelling in a suitcase with unkempt colleagues with unsavoury habits, or social injustice on a global scale, then you might want to pause and contemplate if a more subjective approach would give your film an extra dimension and stimulus, perhaps even adding the occasional touch of humour to alleviate the day-to-day stresses and strains. Issues might even arise during the tour that have been bubbling under the surface, ready to detonate without warning; friction between the band members or dissatisfaction with the roadies, or even the manager; disgruntled fans feeling that the band has lost its way, producing dull and uninspiring work that will eventually make everyone lose interest, with calamitous financial implications.

Such areas of conflict in your film should not be surrendered lightly, but you must never lose sight of the fact that it is only human nature for people to 'act up' when a camera is pointed at them – particularly those who are self-opinionated or have inflated egos. Such scenes might risk appearing contrived and tacky if not handled properly, ultimately damaging your objective to paint an accurate and truthful picture of life on the road. In these instances, the relationship, and trust, that you build up with your subjects will contribute greatly to the film's overall success and this should never be underestimated.

The driving force

The narrative for this particular film, then, is either driven by the sights and sounds that explode in our faces on our journey of discovery, or by the band, the roadies, the manager and the punters giving their views as the story unfolds. You may, however, decide at rough-cut stage that certain vital information is missing that is needed to tie all the strands of the narrative together. The film at this point might, for instance, give no indication of distances between venues, the number of hours spent travelling and performing, the dwindling bookings as the tour progresses, or a dramatic confrontation that is looming between the financiers and the band at the final venue. None of this has been captured adequately during interview sessions to explain it because, frankly, there were far more impromptu and exciting events cascading all around you at every stage of filming. There might even be sub-plots involving groupies accusing members of the band of inappropriate behaviour, police being called to investigate complaints of smashed-up hotel rooms, the lead singer being detained for drunk and disorderly behaviour in some one-horse town in the middle of nowhere and desperately trying to catch up with the main entourage before the next show begins.

The choices available are to either dispense with those particular elements of the story – a clear compromise – or to arrange new interview sessions with the band in order to shore up the gaps, or record an economical, selective narration that will not only effectively fuse the elements together but give the story some much needed dramatic intrigue and suspense.

Placing subjective thoughts within an observational narrative

In D A Pennebaker's 1965 film of Bob Dylan's tour of the UK we observe life on the road with Dylan's entourage through a series of behind-the-scenes vignettes; in taxis, on trains, in hotel rooms and backstage at performances. The film gives us an interesting insight into how performers adapt to such a nomadic lifestyle, yet the camera simply observes Dylan chatting and rehearsing, making no direct comments to camera, and with the film-maker not attempting to influence, or intrude on, the natural progression of events. Pennebaker balances this up by filming the press interviews, during which Dylan opens up and gives us a much better insight into what makes him tick. The film is not subjective, in that Dylan's comments do not drive the story forward, but at least we come away with an impression of how artists cope with several weeks of touring, and the benefit of understanding Dylan a little better than we would if the film had remained purely observational.

Be prepared and save disappointment

Many directors feel that, in hindsight, they might have made a better film if they had been given more time or been better prepared. Earlier I discussed the importance of giving yourself options and being organised and disciplined in order to help overcome certain problems. Obviously you can weigh up some of your options at edit stage and in some cases even improve – or save – your film. But not always. If you keep in mind that your preparation is the greatest investment you can make in your film, you will give yourself the best possible chance of coming through with a successful end product. And although it is not always possible to foresee exactly what is going to happen once you set off with a camera under your arm, thorough research will go a long way in helping you decide what all the possible scenarios and alternatives are so that you can plan accordingly.

YOUR PERSONAL APPROACH

Something that will ultimately determine your approach is the basic genre category your film will fall into. Although drama and documentary are very different in style and technique they can nevertheless retain many of the same genre elements, from action adventure to romantic intrigue, from matters of social concern to the highly comical or downright sarcastic. You may feel, for instance, that more humour can be squeezed from a story by employing a witty narration, or that an investigative piece will be much more powerful if the action is left to speak for itself, with raw, undiluted confrontation.

MAKING YOUR FILM WORK AT MORE THAN ONE LEVEL

Your next task is to decide if your film will employ one technique or several. If the budget for your rock band film is reasonable, you might want to incorporate some imaginative fantasy musical playback sequences running in parallel with the main, more down-to-earth narrative. Such sequences could then be visually 'treated' in the edit suite to give them even greater separation. Adopting a method of integrating two or more very different styles is not confined to this type of scenario, of course. Flashback scenes in either drama or documentary, or reconstruction scenes, can be very effective if planned properly, are relevant to the narrative, and executed with flair.

Counterpoint moves the action forward

And never underestimate the power of counterpoint to reinforce
the spine of your story, or to create more dynamic edit points. In
Power of Love a woman walks through a park recollecting an earlier
love affair. In momentary and 'grainy' flashback we see her as a
younger girl being pushed forward on a swing by her then lover.
As the swing moves forward into shot we cut back to the woman
walking alone in the park in the present day. The swing enters
foreground, now empty – reinforcing the lonely, empty life she
now has, whilst creating a dramatic action 'follow through' of the
swing. Counterpoint can be used in numerous ways – cutting from
a spiritual scene of a martial arts expert practising his moves by a
tranquil lake, for example, to a more aggressive combat scenario,
full of grunts, groans and body thumps, using the movement of
an arm or a hand to effect the cut. In this example we do not
simply contrast action, but also sound, and the edit is all the more
effective for implementing both as a complementary force.

However you choose to employ counterpoint, remember that it
may not always be easy to make such transitions in the edit suite if
you have not planned these scenarios prior to filming. Imagining
scenes in your head and carefully considering your options will
open your mind to a wealth of possibilities long before you start
running videotape through your camera.

Create light and shade

How you texture your film is another important consideration,
which we shall revisit in a later chapter on editing. Texturing
simply means you should always ensure that your film – drama or
documentary – does not run at one continuous level, but ebbs and
flows, sometimes with surprise elements, to keep the audience

interested and fully stimulated. Many a film or video editor has rescued a project from an untimely demise by juxtaposing shots and scenes in order to make the structure of the narrative more interesting and appealing. That may be by slowing or quickening the edit rate, sometimes with music or other sounds; holding back imagery or information to give greater impact, or inter-cutting scenes in a different way in order to either heighten dramatic tension or to give the audience a breather from it.

Bear in mind, though, that an editor can only work with the material at his disposable, so the more you can pre-visualise the ebb and flow of your presentation, and film the elements accordingly, the better chance you will have of making its textured surface more effective when shuffling the images around in the edit suite.

But a film can work at more than one level whatever the subject matter, and whatever its genre. *Around the World in 80 Days* is light entertainment but the series explores other people's cultures, whilst its narrative is a race against time. Simon Chambers' documentary *The Company We Keep* investigates the dubious activities of the Rio Tinto organisation but involves numerous devices to hold the viewers' attention; a combination of traditional investigative storytelling with a more off-the-wall approach, serious reportage mixed with humorous encounters to ensure that it never takes itself too seriously.

Engage your audience from the outset

Audiences can be fickle and hugely demanding. You do not need to start your film with an explosive, action-packed scene that turns their knuckles white as they grip the sides of their seats, but you should, at least, make those opening couple of minutes interesting enough to hold their attention and ease them into the story. As we shall see in Chapter 16, all kinds of tricks can be employed to reel your audience in at the editing stage, but, as before, there will only be so much material you can play with, so thinking about those opening moments prior to filming could prove very advantageous. Remember the opening visuals of a lifeless Jonny Kennedy in *The Boy Whose Skin Fell Off* as he invites us to journey with him through his life, followed by scenes of him gliding through the clouds, as if in a world beyond. It is pointless sitting in the cutting room or edit suite thinking, in retrospect, what a good idea *that* would have been if only you'd thought of it earlier.

A BALANCED VIEWPOINT

A film's balance is not always relative to its technical application or aesthetics. When you have a particular point to make, or axe to grind, or just have a burning desire to make a statement about a particular issue or concern, it is very easy to alienate your audience by coming on too strong. Because you feel passionately about something does not mean you have to beat your audience about the head with a stick or bludgeon them into submission in order to get your views across. This could well have the reverse effect and is entirely unnecessary when you consider how much more rewarding it is to use your skills as a film-maker. Substitute antagonistic interviews and clumsy visual ideas with more subtly crafted cinematic techniques wherever possible and employ a combination of imaginative ideas and subtext to enable your film to work at multiple levels.

This does not mean you have to appear completely impartial to events as, say, news reporters would be expected to be, but you are far more likely to gain audience sympathy with your viewpoint if you show that you have weighed up both sides of an argument and given an opportunity to all parties to have their say. Making a film about a public grievance against the government but without any response from a government spokesman, for instance, might appear unbalanced unless the government was given the opportunity to respond, but declined.

Large corporations often come under fire from film-makers for engaging in dubious and under-handed activities, but if your film has no corporate representation you risk appearing under-researched at best, or indulging in a contrived and biased piece of work at worst. When *The World at War* went into production it was decided that people from all walks of life, be they military commanders, ordinary citizens, politicians, the French Resistance, or members of Hitler's Third Reich, be given a voice, because the viewer should have the right to assess the facts and evaluate the situation for themselves, even though, in this instance, events have a defined historical perspective.

Keeping an open mind

Whilst we are aware of the horrors perpetrated by various people in various situations, or appalled at the actions people take that are beyond our comprehension, it is also important to understand why they happened and how they happened. By giving such perpetrators a voice – be it through a piece of fiction or a documentary – we do at least have the opportunity to assess the situation for ourselves. It might even give us a greater understanding of what brought them to do something so inexplicable – an opportunity that might otherwise have been denied to us.

Freedom of expression is vital in any democratic society. Naturally, you could make a film that is completely subjective on the basis that someone else has the right to make their own film expressing an opposing viewpoint – but should you be so threatened by the possible validity and persuasiveness of such an opposing opinion that it prompts you not to include it in your film in case it damages your own standpoint?

Whilst some might argue that anyone who makes a film has an opinion on the subject and is therefore automatically biased, it boils down to a matter of how you approach the filming and the representation of your subject matter. In many cases it is perfectly legitimate for someone to make a film without a clear viewpoint, since the journey of discovery itself is the very point of making the film in the first place. Film can be a very persuasive and influential medium. I would like to think that the majority of film-makers are prepared to adopt an open mind on most things pertaining to the world at large.

CAN YOUR FILM DRAW A CONCLUSION?

Audiences have an expectation that any film they watch will, in some way, tie up loose ends and bring matters to a conclusion. This is not always the case. Some films leave audiences to make up their own minds as to what might happen next, but if your film does not, or cannot, be fully rounded, the narrative should at least be executed with imagination and flair by way of compensation.

Despite modern techniques of jump-cutting action, leapfrogging chronology, employing split-screen to show parallel scenes, and inter-cutting flashbacks and flash forwards, it is not advisable to leave the audience filling in gaps that you should have filled in for them. The writer Charlie Kaufman confounds and confuses his audience with every work of fiction he produces, but the pieces of the jigsaw ultimately make sense, even if the audience has to work that much harder to piece them together. And because films like *Eternal Sunshine of the Spotless Mind* are so masterfully engineered by writer, director and editor, most of us would be prepared to overlook any areas of confusion because we have been so thoroughly and imaginatively entertained.

Using intrigue to engage your audience

John Lundberg's NFTS film *The Mythologist* explores the strange Walter Mitty world of Armen Victorian, a seemingly ordinary guy living with his wife and two children in Nottingham, working, it is rumoured, as an insurance salesman or shop assistant. Armen's other occupations, however, form part of a more sinister and murky world, from diplomat to UFO investigator, adventurer to crop circle researcher. Most intriguingly, Armen Victorian is such an extremely difficult person to find, we would actually believe him to be a myth if so many of the people interviewed in the film had not actually met him.

Lundberg spends much of the film attempting to track down Victorian, corresponding with him via email and answering questions as to why he wants to meet up and film him. The finale to the film is an email from Victorian to the director thanking him for taking an interest in him as a subject for a documentary but, on careful consideration, he has decided not to go ahead with it. Whilst we, as viewers, therefore never actually meet Armen Victorian, we do not feel for one moment let down, because Lundberg tells his story with imagination, laced with more than a dash of intrigue, using stylish imagery and the email device –

whether true or contrived – to build the tension and link the various scenarios involving spies, spooks, subterfuge and the revelation of secrets. In truth, meeting Armen may even have turned out to be a terrible disappointment, exploding a myth that might not have lived up to the ingenuity of the storytelling.

CHOOSING YOUR SUBJECT MATTER

For a first film you naturally want to make as an effective and workmanlike job as possible. You may already have a drama script or a subject in mind that you are passionate about and are completely focused on making your film around. If not, I offer the following advice:

- Write down five different subject headings that you feel could make a compelling story, possibly making each one different in style and approach, be that investigative, humorous, comedy, horror, adventure, stylised or whatever. Then draw up a list of the separate components that you feel will be needed to tell that story with conviction and accuracy and engage our attention from start to finish. Assess which of the five could work at more than one level and offer you the most potential for texturing both subject matter and visual imagery.

- If it is a mini drama, and your first film, make it a contemporary piece to avoid having to make accurate historical references with regard to make-up, wardrobe and props. Select or write a story with a strong structure that is original and not clichéd, has a unique voice, and will work without being over-loaded with dialogue and multiple twists, or cluttered with large numbers of characters entering and exiting frame. Consider how your idea can be turned into a striking visual narrative using a clearly defined style that is not overly complicated. The books of Syd Field, William Goldman and Robert McKee give excellent pointers on the art of screenwriting, even though your script should ultimately be an original work of self-expression.

■ If your film is factual, contact the people you would like to film and find out if they will give their permission. If these people are to drive the narrative but are not interested in being filmed, or have absolutely no on-screen charisma, you do not have a film. Or if you approach property owners and local authorities for permission to film at a desired location but are refused, you may not have a film, depending on its importance to the story and whether you can replace it. In other words, begin with a vision, then narrow it down to the practicalities, adapting the concept with the least amount of compromise possible – or move on to option two.

Discover what other film-makers are doing

Before making a final decision it would be advantageous to look at some of the many hundreds of short films that are available for viewing at the click of a mouse on the web. The range and depth of these films is staggering and will give you an excellent idea of the different stories, styles and techniques being adopted by up and coming film-makers.

The BBC's excellent website, film network at www.bbc.co.uk/filmnetwork has a film-making guide and various short films you can watch online, as does Channel Four's Four Docs at www.channel4.com/fourdocs, www.channel4.com/film/shortsand clips, the young film-makers network at www.cineclub.org.uk, international films at www.atomfilms.com, YouTube at www.you tube.com and MySpace at www.myspace.com.

Whilst some of the above show user-generated content and home-produced films among their offerings, there are numerous websites, such as the British Film Institute at www.bfi.org.uk/ filmdownloads.html where, for a small fee, you can download classic shorts and features to watch. It is also worth contacting some of the film schools to see if you can obtain any DVD copies of recent student films, many of which are of an exceptionally high standard.

A further possibility is to check out specialist screenings at the National Film Theatre or clubs and societies nationwide; events and film programmes being listed in local and national newspapers and on their own websites.

As a matter of course you should immerse yourself in the culture of film at every opportunity, on television and at the cinema. By observing the professionals you will discover a valuable and diverse brew of experience and innovation that will be the catalyst for the evaluation and exploration of a rich and endless seam of possibility.

6

Nothing is What it Seems

Because we are such unpredictable and complex creatures, human beings will always have the ability to surprise or shock. You can walk down any street in any town, looking intently into the faces of those coming towards you, but you will not truly know what is really going on beneath the surface. Most of us are chameleons when it comes to social interaction, adapting our personalities to suit certain circumstances, or the people we are with at any particular time. Little wonder that sometimes we know so little about the people we share an office with, or even our friends, since most of us go about our daily business revealing very little of our inner selves, often disguising pain, deviousness, corruption, perversion, deceit, tragedy and personal torment.

DISCOVERING THE TRUTH

As a film-maker you have a rare opportunity to strip away the outer veneer and scratch beneath the sensory surface in order to discover the truth, opening our eyes to what is really going on around us and challenging us to see things in a different light. A film that does not give us any new insights into the characters within it, or only tells us what we can outwardly see, or already know, risks becoming mediocre and unadventurous, with little to captivate or engage us, or prompt us to ask questions to which we want answers.

Exploring beneath the sensory surface

The text of a film – that which we can see in terms of action, dialogue, sounds – is something we can almost reach out and touch. The subtext – the inner thoughts and feelings that disguise behaviour, true thoughts and feelings, tensions, personal agendas or desires – runs in parallel to the main text, bubbling under the surface, until we, the audience, make a connection between the two – which, if timed properly, becomes a moment of true revelation and understanding.

Subtext works well in drama because writers can carefully craft the two levels, whereas in documentary we are at the mercy of real life events as they unfold around us, not always wanting to play ball with our master plan, and although documentary does not necessarily rely on any form of subtext to make it work, drama almost certainly does.

SUBTEXT IN DRAMA

In *The Sixth Sense* Bruce Willis plays a social do-gooder, Dr Malcolm Crowe, who has an obsession with his work as a child psychologist. In the opening scene his wife's casual remark about how he puts everything else second, including her, suggests an undercurrent of discontent, even though she clearly loves her husband. In the following scene they discover an intruder in their bedroom – a former patient who feels that Crowe has let him down and who, in a fit of anger, shoots him.

Fast forward one year and we now find Crowe trying to help a young boy called Cole, a clearly disturbed individual who, among other things, talks to dead people, much to the dismay of his mother. The scenes with Crowe attempting to make contact with

Cole establish that the doctor is still fixated with his work, so much so that when he turns up late at a restaurant for an anniversary dinner with his wife, she ignores him and walks off.

The perception and the reality

That is the text of the film. What the writer/director M. Night Shyamalan presents to us is a fanatical man who is risking his marriage for his work and possibly putting his life in danger for a second time, to the extent that the love she once had for him has now burned out and turned to hate.

The subtext, however, comes as a shocking revelation when Crowe returns home in the final scene to discover his distraught wife on the sofa, exhausted from another crying session. As she drops the wedding ring she has been clutching and it rolls across the floor, he holds up his hand and we realise that it is not *her* ring on the floor, but his – no longer on its rightful place on his finger.

In that one moment of revelation, two strands of subtext collide head on as we realise that Crowe has actually been dead for most of the film, killed by the assailant in the opening scene, and that his wife is not filled with hate for him, but a burning love, coupled with a devastating sense of loss, that she cannot come to terms with. Crowe, who up to now has refused to face up to the reality of the situation, is finally able to step back and allow her to put her life back together again.

This is highly emotive stuff, made more powerful by a subtext that moves forward in unison with the main text, making us reflect on the difficulties that human beings have with regard to confronting the problems of relationships, death, loss, eternal love and commitment – not just with partners and spouses, but between parent and child.

SUBTEXT IN DOCUMENTARY

Whilst a documentary film-maker cannot construct subtext in the same way, there are many instances where it can strengthen a story. A film about a sky-diving school, for instance, involving a bunch of daredevils who swap stories of bravado in the local pub and jump from aeroplanes without a second thought for their safety – until we discover that one of them is actually terrified of participating in the sport and has an ulterior motive in trying to overcome a basic fear of heights, or is trying to win friends by appearing to be something that he is not.

Or perhaps a film portrait of a singer/songwriter who has an amazing talent and a huge following, but for some reason has never hit the big time in terms of international fame and financial reward. She is always smiling for the cameras during rehearsals and performances, not once dropping her guard about the dark times she has endured. Although she harbours regrets about her failure to fulfil her professional desires she finally reveals, during interview, that a near brush with death and the recent birth of her daughter have put her life back in perspective and made her aware of the things that are truly important in her life.

In both instances the film-maker has peeled away the outer façade and questioned what is really going on, devising a narrative in which the underlying strand to the story supports the main text to maximum effect.

Going beyond the obvious

Perhaps the most difficult task you face as a film-maker is to make your work so engaging and exclusive that it stands out from the crowd whilst retaining strong artistic style and substance. Anyone can pick up a camera and film an exciting and entertaining sequence for, say, a Formula One motor race, by shooting a variety of angles of screeching tyres and cars hurtling past camera, then editing them together with fast-paced music. But thousands of films have been made this way and, no matter how professional they look, they work primarily at the one level of visual stimulation.

By looking beyond the obvious and identifying a subtext you might discover that your story has numerous layers that can be explored: a driver who feels that age is catching up with him and the pressure to stay on top creates greater and riskier challenges; or a deep-rooted rivalry between drivers that either creates dramatic tension or encourages reckless behaviour that may have ramifications for work colleagues and families alike.

The fusion of picture and sound in a colourful kaleidoscope of events is pointless and commonplace unless you can reach in and pull out something that is more meaningful. An awareness of how ruthless ambition might ultimately destroy a human being, or how human endeavour can succeed against all the odds, are just two examples of elements that can take your film beyond the obvious and allow your audience the benefit of deeper emotional involvement and fulfilment.

USING EXPOSITION

The placement of exposition in your narrative – the information the audience needs to understand fully what is going on – is crucial to the successful telling of the story and can also make the subtext that much stronger. But exposition given as direct information to the audience without any attempt at disguising or concealing it can appear heavy-handed and clumsy and often impair the impact of your film.

Exposition working directly with subtext

In the drama short *Rocko's Story*, about a hoodlum terrorising people in the East End of London, important information about the troubled background of the main character is held back until the end of the film. If the director had felt we needed to know about Rocko's problems from the outset he might have opted to use a voice-over to introduce the character and explain about him being a little weird because his father was an alcoholic who continually abused him. Or placed two onlookers sitting in a bar making the observation: 'There goes old Rocko, daft as a brush, pity he suffered such abuse by his father as a child.'

Neither examples are very subtle and virtually wreck any possibility for dramatic intrigue because we would know right from the outset that Rocko's tough guy act hides a deeper insecurity that he is battling to overcome. By concealing this information from the audience until the final scene we misinterpret Rocko's behaviour patterns. In the end scene where Rocko is finally driven to despair and threatens to knife his brother, the sibling empathises with Rocko, revealing that he knows all about what their father did, forcing Rocko to confront his demons in an emotional outpouring that causes him to break down and reveal himself as a weak individual in desperate need of help.

We are given exactly the same information, only this time at the *end* of the film and not the beginning, and the exposition is integrated into a dramatic situation, creating a dilemma as to whether the brother will live or die. It is only then that we realise we have been wrong in our assumptions about Rocko.

Exposition in documentary

Sometimes it is important to give the audience vital information from the start of a film – 'Jonny Kennedy is dead but he is also very much alive' or the device used in *The Company we Keep* to tell us about Simon Chambers' quest to discover the truth about Rio Tinto; exposition in the form of a diary to his (fictional) grandmother who has left him shares in the organisation. When Chambers writes a diary entry to her at the end of the film thanking her, but declining her gift, it is likely he is really saying to us: 'I have investigated the Rio Tinto organisation and found it culpable'. In this example we know the nature of the quest from the outset, but there is absolutely no reason why, in some instances, documentary cannot hold back exposition to make the story more engaging and revealing in the same way that drama can.

In the 1970 short, *Just Another Day*, John the down-and-out busker entertains West End crowds, singing and playing his banjo. John is not the most accomplished of musicians but passing pedestrians are so charmed by his personable manner and optimism in the face of adversity that they willingly fill his hat with loose change. What they – and we – do not realise is that John is not homeless at all, but lives in a respectable end-of-terrace house in Neasden, to which he returns at the end of the film. In the first edit of *Just Another Day* John is seen leaving his house on his way to 'work' but the director decided that too much information was being given too soon and that this piece of exposition should be moved from the front of the film to the end.

Charlotte Boulay-Goldsmith's excellent 2005 documentary short, *Clowns Don't Cry*, tells the story of a man who spends his days entertaining families in Covent Garden dressed as a clown. As we watch him perform magic tricks and create animals from balloons, we wonder what motivates him to leave his home in Milton Keynes every morning and travel to London to take on this somewhat unconventional persona. His voice-track offers some clues. As a boy he loved the circus and his hero was Coco the Clown. He has many friends who work in show business – so is this a lost vocation perhaps? He talks of the joys of giving and receiving love and since he clearly enjoys putting on a show for the kids, we simply assume that he is just a well-meaning eccentric.

Until, that is, two thirds into the film he tells us that his ex-wife once told him that clowning was the second woman, and a few moments later the revelation that they adopted a Downs Syndrome baby who had almost died. By placing these two important pieces of exposition towards the end of the film they become a poignant revelation and we now see the character as a lonely figure who has endured much sadness in his life. To make people laugh you need to know what makes them cry, he tells us as he makes his way home at the end of the day, and we have complete empathy for his situation.

In these examples the sections of exposition put at the front of the stories would have effectively destroyed the subtext and both films would have played at just one level, their impact on the story quite possibly being significantly lessened.

How film-makers can change perceptions

All of the examples discussed in this chapter are in some ways relative to the discovery of truth, a fundamental requirement for the likes of John Grierson when he made some of the earliest documentaries on record as far back as 1926.

Seeing the light

Objective or observational filming, although informative, does not puncture the sensory surface in the same way that subjective filming can. Yet whilst truth presents us with the facts, *enlightenment* goes beyond truth to reveal the emotional ramifications and far-reaching consequences of our actions. The truth is fact. Enlightenment is what we learn from the revelation of a given situation or set of circumstances.

Our changing perceptions and attitudes are a part of the natural process of enlightenment and film-makers can create awareness whilst helping to influence those perceptions. Imagine what those crowds parading on Brighton seafront in all their finery in 1900 would have made of the thousands of football supporters chanting on the terraces in their jeans and trainers in *The Score*. A world away, yet film enables us to hold a mirror up to our society and make the comparison between two distinctly different lifestyles and attitudes, one equally unbelievable to the other.

Films, whether drama or documentary, can have high emotional impact on their audience, particularly when the viewer can relate them to personal experiences.

In the NFTS film *The Secret*, the main character Arthur suffers from Obsessive Compulsive Disorder, which in his case means he has to count everything in threes. The film is another excellent example of integrating visual stylisation into a more serious narrative, with numerous visual examples of the number three invading our senses as Arthur tells his distressing story.

In 1900 it's likely that Arthur would have been locked up for behaving in such a weird and inexplicable manner, in the same way that autistic children would have been humiliated or beaten because they were perceived as just behaving badly. Today we know that autism and OCD are serious problems affecting thousands of children and adults – and thanks to the work of doctors, psychiatrists and film-makers, we have been significantly enlightened.

7

Mixing Your Ingredients

Whatever kind of film you want to make, and whatever techniques you wish to employ, you will be crafting and refining a piece of work that contains a particular combination of component parts.

DECIDING ON YOUR FILM'S COMPONENTS

The order in which you eventually film your shots and scenes will almost certainly not be your final edited running order. Since it is all too easy to occasionally lose sight of the film's objectives once your brain is hijacked by other essentials, such as setting up locations and tracking down interviewees, it is always useful to stay focused in whatever way you can.

Formulating a list of your film's components is a positive and constructive starting point, as these will not only concentrate your mind on what elements are relevant to the narrative, but how these elements might work when put together. They could be any combination of:

■ studio shoots
■ set builds
■ props
■ sound playback
■ location footage and establishers
■ observational (real time) footage

- interviews or vox pops (in vision or sound recordings only)
- voice narration
- bluescreen
- archive footage
- photographs or press cuttings
- music
- actors for a drama or drama reconstruction scenes
- background extras
- wardrobe and costume
- graphics.

STUDIO BOUND

The first observation with regard to studio filming is the cost factor. Whilst a studio is a controlled environment allowing maximum flexibility over lighting, sound and continuity, the costs can rise as you begin to factor in set-builds and props, ongoing refurbishment such as painting or rebuilds, make-up and wardrobe rooms and use of office space, photocopiers and telephones. If your shoot is either non-synch or to sound playback, it is probably not necessary to hire a sound stage, in which case a photographic studio may meet your requirements, but you need to weigh up the advantages and disadvantages. Synch sound is not necessary if you are recording a song to playback, for example, but any spoken sections of dialogue mimed to a pre-recorded voice-track (unless they are puppets or animatronics) would risk looking suspiciously post-dubbed, and you would be well advised not to pursue that particular route.

ON LOCATION

Since filming in a studio might prove to be a costly exercise, first-time film-makers – particularly those not filming any drama scenes needing set construction – would be advised to utilise exterior and interior locations as much possible, if not exclusively.

In Chapters 8 and 9 we will look in more detail at the implications of location filming with regard to scheduling and permissions. Essentially, you need to find a location that is both suitable and relevant to your production – be it fiction or documentary – then establish the virtues and drawbacks of that location with regard to factors such as geography and noise, health and safety, and whether you need permission to film there, regardless of whether it is public or private property. This is very important, since the last thing you need in the middle of a hectic filming schedule is to be asked to leave a location because you did not check if any clearances were required.

Stay lightweight

And you will need to take into account how lightweight you may need to be once you take to the road. Transporting heavy lights, gels and lighting stands around with you – and possibly a generator to power the lights – is not the most efficient way to film a fly-on-the-wall documentary. Set-up time also has to be taken into account, so you should consider if interior locations such as halls and clubs have adequate natural lighting and if you can schedule such shoots during daylight hours. Taking a reflector with you on location will certainly improve your chances of reflecting light onto an area where it is most needed, particularly faces.

Decide whether to shoot sound with picture

Interviews are often filmed in the subject's garden, or study, and you'll need to decide if you actually need to run film or videotape during an interview, or just record the sound. Although a simple voice recording will save you a lot of camera set-up time, you should be absolutely sure that the subject will never appear on camera or you could find yourself regretting the decision once you start piecing everything together in the edit suite, and you have no adequate cutaways to support a vital section of sound track.

CREATING AN ILLUSION

Working with special effects is a highly specialised area and you would do well to give them a wide berth for a first film and concentrate on creating a strong and engaging narrative. In certain circumstances, however, you may want to consider using bluescreen, a method by which foreground elements such as an interview are filmed against a blue, or green, screen and a new background is 'keyed' in later during the edit process. Chromakey, as it is known, can sometimes be very useful for relatively straightforward applications, particularly interviews.

You might want to film an interview with someone discussing the problems of traffic or air pollution. Whilst filming in a relevant environment would lend an authentic air, you would be flirting with disaster even if you were allowed to film the interview by the side of a motorway or runway with all its distractions and noise, when a controlled environment would produce better sound quality and be a good deal safer.

Integrating your subject into the visualisation

You might feel that your subject matter would benefit from some interesting visual interplay, such as a presenter or an interviewee, standing (or sitting) inside a doll's house for a historical perspective on hobbies and crafts. Or relevant action being keyed in behind an interviewee for a documentary on, say, magic, with performances taking place behind the subject, or as a hologram on a table in the foreground – or both. In the BBC series *Comics Brittania*, a history of British comics from the late 1930s, all the interviewees are placed inside a selection of comic strips, integrating them into the subject matter in a fun and imaginative way. These sequences are intercut with photographs of the early cartoonists and sepia reconstructions of kids reading comics, along with archive footage of children playing in the streets in the 1940s and 50s, in order to create a highly effective and atmospheric blend of the old and the new.

Whatever its application, whether for practical reasons or just for fun, you need to tread very carefully when you use chromakey because the background needs to be lit evenly in order to avoid any shadowing that will make the keying difficult, or cause 'fringeing' around the foreground. The set-up time can also make serious inroads into your schedule. Avoid if at all possible.

DELVING INTO THE ARCHIVES

A documentary – and sometimes even a work of fiction – often has the need for some film library footage. In such instances it might be wise to research the availability of the footage you need before filming, in case it is either unsuitable or not available – otherwise you may have to complete your film without it or adjust your shot material accordingly.

The advantage of viewing library footage in advance is that you can actually schedule shots and scenes to cross-edit with that footage, even building in some visual counter-pointing or match-edits. Dissolving from a street scene in present-day Piccadilly Circus to the same scene in 1880 might be visually more effective if you can match the scene from a similar camera position, which is only possible if you have the archive shot to work from. For a drama or drama documentary you may also need to match clothes, uniforms and props to the original, rather than second guessing what they might be when you eventually track down the archive material.

Clearing copyright on archive material

Archive footage is, of course, copyright protected, and therefore costly, depending on the specialised nature of its content. Many film archives sell their footage by the minute, or part thereof, which can be prohibitively expensive if you are hoping to sell your film for an international audience and have to pay up front. Paying world rights for footage used in a film that may not be seen outside of its country of origin would be hugely optimistic, so it may come down to your powers of negotiation with the copyright owner, or in some cases the estate of the copyright owner.

You may be able to agree an initial search fee and pay for the duplication of the material, or perhaps for the domestic rights, on the understanding that payment would be made if worldwide sales are agreed and you have a distribution deal in place. Most broadcasters – including regional broadcasters – have an archive department with a rate card, as do many independents and specialist organisations. *The Moving History* website, for example, lists many organisations in the UK that you can contact with regard to archive footage, including:

- The British Film Institute
- The Imperial War Museum
- East Anglian Film Archive
- Media Archive for Central England
- Yorkshire Film Archive
- Scottish Screen Archives.

The Researcher's Guide Online (RGO) has entries in some 550 film, television, radio and related documentation collections in the UK and Ireland, including national and regional archives and stockshot libraries, and collections held by education establishments, museums, local authorities, corporations and private collectors. ITN not only has its own archive but also manages the vast British Pathé News collection. Getty Images has a huge resource, as does the BBC Motion Gallery and British Movietone News, and virtually every country in the world has its own film archives, a comprehensive list of which can be accessed at The Public Moving Images Archive. An amazing selection of stockshot footage can also be located on the internet through any search engine simply by keying in 'stockshot libraries'.

Many of the above organisations will also have photo libraries. Magazines and newspapers, both national and local, are another obvious source of finding photographic imagery, along with press headlines or cuttings that may be needed to 'fill in' some gaps in your story. Typical photo libraries you can contact include Camera Press, the ITN Archive, the National Trust, the Nature Picture Library and Image Source. The British Association of Picture Libraries and Agencies also has an online database through which you can search literally thousands of photographs, all listed in specific categories.

THE POWER OF MUSIC

Most directors and editors will tell you just how powerful and motivational the addition of music can be to your film, if used in the right way. In Chapter 12 we will look at some examples of how music can enhance your film but for the moment we will examine the four basic types of music, and the implications and benefits in using each.

- Your own music.
- Commercial music.
- Specially composed music.
- Library music.

All music, as with archive film and photographs, is copyright protected. There is nothing to stop you composing your own soundtrack if you are handy with a guitar or piano, or have friends in a band who are keen to extend their range of musical talents and ideas, but you should think seriously about registering the work with an organisation that deals with protecting your rights, such as the MCPS and PRS, in the event that the film, and its music, were to take off and attract worldwide exposure.

Be careful though. Whilst music can enhance your film it also has the potential to ruin it if used inappropriately, or if it interferes with dialogue and other important elements of the soundtrack. Just because a piece of music is cheap or available is not a good enough reason to put it in your film.

Commercial music – i.e. the kind that you can purchase at any music store on CD or DVD – may well add something special to your film, perhaps because of a certain set of lyrics, or because the tune is universally known, but it is extremely expensive, even if you only want to include a small section in your movie. Although you may have purchased the CD it still needs to be cleared for public broadcasting. To clear a commercial recording you need a synchronisation licence from the publisher and a licence from the owner of the sound recording.

You may have to negotiate a price, dependant on its usage, and you could well be looking at mega money if the film is to be distributed internationally.

Making music work in harmony with your film

Specially composed music can, in some instances, be just as costly, or more so, particularly if you are using a well-known composer who insists on using a full orchestra to record the score. There is no question, however, that in most cases a scored soundtrack will take your film to another level, adding an extra layer of drama and tension, making us feel good about the characters or the storyline itself, increasing and slowing the pace, or reducing us to tears. Music can be such an emotive force, in fact, that if you stripped the music from your finished film, you would be amazed at just how powerful its presence had been – even if, for the most part, it had been working at a sub-conscious level.

Not all film composers come at a high price, of course, but although there are hundreds of good musicians who would do an excellent job for you at reasonable cost, the overall budget figure may still have to include additional musicians for the recording and royalty payments on subsequent usage, such as soundtrack releases, worldwide sales or DVD distribution. It is often possible to negotiate a buyout payment with the composer, and specially composed music is cleared through the commissioning agreement, which may or may not include the clearance of any performance on the recordings.

Music is an extremely versatile complement to your film but it does not always need to be a swirling, ravenously sensual masterpiece. Some scenes might work best with a single discordant piano, or a violin, or a rarely heard instrument that is not terribly melodic but produces a haunting sound that can have extraordinary impact on a scene. And many musicians, working alone in their own mini recording studios, can produce staggering works simply by using a synthesiser and a gloriously fertile musical mind, and these musical geniuses are certainly worth their weight in gold.

Music off the shelf

Royalty-free music is a collection of pre-recorded music that has no additional licence fees to pay once a music track has been purchased. Various music libraries, however, have conditions attached, such as restricted use in advertising, additional payments for bulk production, and broadcast television.

The downside of using library music is that you will probably have to sift your way through hours of inappropriate, very-similar-sounding tracks before you come across that perfect little gem, and then there's always the possibility that hundreds of other directors have used the same track in their own films. However, music libraries worldwide have been in existence for a very long time and the catalogue of choice is both vast and enterprising, with music supplied by some top-notch musicians – and it certainly is the most cost-effective way of incorporating professional music into your soundtrack.

Among the more established music libraries in the UK are De Wolfe, KPM, Atmosphere Music, The Beat Suite, Cavendish Music Library, Bruton Music, Carlin Production Music, Chappell Recorded Music Library, Red Bus Music and Primrose Music, and there are many more you can check out on the internet. By registering online at many of these websites you can listen to a range of tracks and then download your preferred choice.

The authorisation process with regard to library music is relatively painless since both the use of the music copyright and the sound recording is cleared through one licence. You simply submit a music cue sheet to the music library, listing the details of any tracks used so that royalties can be paid to the composer.

WORKING WITH ACTORS

If you are making a drama or a drama documentary you will need actors in your production. For a first film you might want to dip a toe in the water by recruiting friends and family, or visiting your local amateur dramatics group to sound out likely candidates. It is not the ideal solution, but may be a better prospect than not making your film at all. The participants in Kevin Brownlow's *It Happened Here* were predominantly amateurs, and both Peter Watkins and Ken Russell used an amateur cast in *The War Game* and *Amelia and the Angel* respectively, the former receiving a BAFTA and an Oscar.

Don't choose actors just because they are available

Tread carefully, though. You may get away with amateurs being involved as background artists, or in groups, but if you have a script which requires dialogue you should consider involving a professional if at all possible. Acting is a craft that cannot be underestimated and it really could make the difference to the film's success or failure. The same rule of thumb applies as it does with music – using friends as actors because they are free and available is not a good enough reason to put them in your film. Some of them might find it fun to be involved at first, but by take 27 they could well lose the will to live and set off back home – assuming, that is, they turned up in the first place.

Explore all the options

Another option is to approach the various drama schools and academies, such as East 15, Mountview or LAMDA, and check out if anyone might be suitable for your film and be prepared to participate. You might also try contacting some of the film schools to see if they can offer any help, or organisations such as PCR (Production and Casting Report), where film students can place casting ads for free – or browse through a copy of *The Stage* for general theatre and film information, to find out who is doing what, or to place an ad for actors or audition venues. And look for actors with interesting faces as opposed to those who are predictably attractive as they can add extra depth to the characterisations.

Professional actors are a worthy investment

On first consideration it may appear that professional actors might bring an assortment of baggage to your production, particularly if you have very little money to spend. There is their basic fee, possible royalties on top of that, and travel and meal expenses. Bear in mind though that many actors are taken advantage of when they are starting out and a huge number do not work for many months. Your on-screen talent is indispensable and although it is only right that your artistes should be treated fairly, you can always negotiate with actors looking, just as you are, for an opportunity to get a foot in the door – and a surprising number, even well-known actors, would often be happy to work on a low budget project with a passionate new director and a good idea.

Approaching an actor

If you decide to approach a professional actor there are a number of possibilities. You could send the script directly to the actor and bypass the agent, assuming you have access, or involve the actor's agent from the beginning. Or you might approach an agency to enquire who they have on their books that might be suitable, and willing, to take on a role. Agents are naturally protective of their clients but if you are able to show yourself to be both committed and honest – and have interesting ideas – the support of an agency could be no bad thing in the long run. Or you could contact *Spotlight*, an organisation with a massive database of acting talent. You can either view actors' details online or through *Spotlight*'s publication, both of which have links to international listings.

Consider a casting director

Budget permitting, you could take the course of most productions and employ a casting director. Casting directors know the agents, they know who's 'hot' and who isn't, and they keep track of all the new emerging talent. If you happen to need three or four actors in your film they would also do the ground work in finding suitable types for the production. In all films involving drama, casting is definitely the key. Get that right and you are already halfway there.

Set up auditions

Wherever you gather your prospective talent from, be it friends, acting academies or agencies, never promise a role until you are absolutely certain you have the right actor for the part, and set up an audition session so that you can properly assess who is the best choice for each role. Ask the actors to read from the script, giving notes wherever possible so that they understand both the storyline and the character they are being asked to play. Take photographs of them and if possible videotape the audition for playing back later. It is surprising how you can forget the strengths and weaknesses of a reading a few days after the event, and a recording gives you the opportunity to make comparisons between the various performances before making a commitment.

And whether your final cast is amateur or professional, you should draw up a contract with anyone who appears in front of camera to protect you legally. Even if you initially set out to make a film as a showpiece for your talents, or just to gain the experience, you might discover that your film actually has sales potential, in which event you will need to make sure you are covered against any possible comebacks.

Allow for rehearsal time

It is always advisable to meet up with your cast several days before filming begins to go through the script and explain your vision, giving them an opportunity to make suggestions and explore the characterisations and subtext. Never expect any actor to turn up on a set or a location and go straight in to their role. By nature, actors are generally a sensitive, insecure and demanding bunch who need reassurance and encouragement – and small wonder when they are expected to arrive on set and pull a terrific performance out of the bag, sometimes in front of a group of people they have never met before.

Give your actors some breathing space so they can go through the script, rehearse their lines, or just chill out. Artists spend more time hanging around during a shoot waiting for lighting and set changes than they do working, so make sure they are comfortable and have a room away from the main activity. And whatever logistical problems you face with the shoot, always make time to keep them in the loop so they know what's going on and do not feel isolated or neglected.

Blocking saves time

You should always allow time for blocking through the shots so that you can see how a scene works best or what problems might be encountered. A tracking shot in a park might suddenly bring a line of modern houses into view during a period drama, or a sensitive romantic moment might be ruined by the sun glinting fiercely into the lens because you selected the wrong camera angle.

Actors can get very irritated if they feel the scene has not been thought through properly and time is being wasted, so work out your shots during the recce if possible, drawing up floor (or ground) plans, no matter how rough, for plotting camera and actor positions later. And always block the scenes through with the actors before filming, whilst lights and sets are being adjusted, for instance – providing you are not in the way or breaching any health and safety regulations.

Remember:

- Do not select friends and family just because they are available.

- Never say never. A professional actor may not be as out of reach as you think.
- Contact drama schools and casting agencies and place ads in trade journals.
- Use a casting director if at all possible.
- Set up auditions and record them for later appraisal.
- Allow time before filming to explain your vision and explore the characters.
- Always give your actors space on set and keep them in the loop.
- Block through the scenes prior to filming.
- Respect your actors. Utilise their energies and skills for everyone's benefit.

The problems of filming out of sequence

Something else to bear in mind when working with actors is that you will inevitably be filming your shots out of sequence order, because it is much easier to schedule shots that are all in one particular direction – i.e. in a bedroom facing a window – followed by all the reverse shots in the opposite direction (reverse angles) – facing, say, the fireplace.

This is great for lighting each camera set-up in one continuous block, but not so great for keeping track of continuity – especially if the reverses are filmed several days later – or for the actors who are often required to play widely disparate scenes one after the other, switching their emotional responses from scene to scene.

Whilst lighting set-ups like this work at their most efficient in a studio, on location there could be changing conditions in natural light between set-ups that you have little or no control over. And if the shooting is spread over several weeks, changing seasonal conditions might also give you serious continuity problems.

FINALISING YOUR COMPONENTS

As you progress through the research phase the components necessary to tell your story will gradually fall into place, some possibly being jettisoned along the way, others being factored into your final story arc.

Finding archive, music, photographs, props and actors can sometimes take what seems an eternity, so you need to learn how to short-cut the process as much as possible. Experience is ultimately the best way, making good reliable contacts another, but buying yourself a copy of a production manual such as *The Knowledge*, *Kemps Production Handbook*, *Kays Production Manual*, or the *Film-makers' Yearbook* will not only provide an extremely valuable resource but save you a great deal of leg-work.

8

Avoiding Unnecessary Complications

Because of the unpredictable nature of filming, with the potential for things not going according to plan and everything becoming just too much to bear thinking about, there is a school of thought that suggests you should throw caution to the wind, go out and make your film and tackle any fallout later. Which is all very well if it is not your money that's being spent and you don't have a delivery deadline to meet.

CLEARING YOUR GROUND

Filming can be complicated enough without adding to your problems, so my advice is to prepare thoroughly and head any potential problems off at the pass before they have a chance to take a bite at you.

There are any number of subjects you may want to tackle and capture on film, from the amazingly simple to the extraordinarily complicated, and every film-maker has the right to express themselves in whatever way they choose, be that entertaining us, bringing social injustice to our attention or exposing political and corporate misdemeanours. As an independent film-maker, however, and without the support and advice of a company's legal advisers, you are somewhat vulnerable and need to clear your ground carefully, especially if your subject matter is likely to be contentious or has legal implications. You do not want to find yourself being ejected from a location, paying huge retrospective financial claims to contributors, or being sued or threatened because you did not check your facts, or stepped over the legal boundaries without even realising it.

FILMING WITH CHILDREN

The tricky challenges in finding actors, auditioning them, casting them and negotiating with them are a stroll in the park compared to using children in a film. They are, quite rightly, a protected specie, and your voyage into young persons' territory will be littered with all kinds of trapdoors.

Depending on their age and experience in front of camera, children can tire very quickly, so the more you can achieve as early as you can, the better, and always allocate extra time for loo visits and fruit-juice breaks. You will also need to allow for rehearsal time if the child has a substantial role in the film, and spend significant time with them on set so that everything can be explained very carefully to them.

Acts and regulations are there for their protection

Whether your film is a full-blown feature, a high-budget documentary, or a low-budget independent production, if the child you want in your film is under 16 you will need the permission of a parent, or those with parental responsibility, and a licence from the local authority where the child lives (not where they will be working). And the child will have to be chaperoned at all times.

Children's participation as performers is strictly regulated, with England, Wales, Scotland and Northern Ireland all having similar but differing legislation, and the interpretation and application of Acts and Regulations can also vary from one local authority to another.

The Children and Young Persons Act applies to:

- any child under minimum school age taking part in performance
- performance on licensed premises
- performance that is for broadcast
- films or presentations for public exhibition.

All children of compulsory school age and under must be licensed, the exception being if no payment is made other than expenses. In these circumstances, as long as the child is not absent from school during term time, no licence is required. You must, however, always complete a child's risk assessment as required by the Management of Health and Safety at Work Regulations – as well as for your own peace of mind.

Adhere to all local authority requirements

The local authority will require a photograph of the child, a description of the nature of the performance, a birth certificate, school clearance forms, a form signed by the film's producer, a form signed by the parents, a form signed by the doctor confirming that the child is fit and healthy, and a letter from the school approving the child's leave of absence if during compulsory schooling and in term time. Some authorities are more flexible than others with regard to having original copies or faxed copies of the documentation, and a licence being made within 21 days from application.

And even when all the paperwork is in place you cannot work children beyond a certain set of hours. In the UK, for a child up to five years old that's five hours a day, for five years to nine years it's seven and a half hours and for nine years and older, nine and a half hours.

For a documentary you will still require a parent or guardian's permission for a child's involvement and you should conceal the faces of any children for whom such permission has not been granted. Permission from the child's school and the local authority may also be required if the child is performing or being directed as opposed to, say, being interviewed in a spontaneous vox pop situation.

Make contact with organisations that can help

If you are casting for a drama, or for a music or dance performance, you would do well to contact a stage school such as the Sylvia Young Theatre School or a child's casting agency such as Whizz Kids. Not only are the children trained in the disciplines of drama, many can dance, sing and play musical instruments; some have experience of working in a professional environment and the organisation will take care of the paperwork. Modelling agencies such as Scallywags can also supply children in speaking and non-speaking roles and save you time and effort by organising licences.

Children have a different perspective

Never forget that child performers do not have the same perspective on things as adults and you will never fully appreciate the true meaning of unpredictability until you film with children.

A few years ago I was working on a children's drama and had to complete a scene with an eight-year-old boy riding a bicycle. Unfortunately, the design department had only managed to supply a pink bike so I apologised and told him that it was the best we could do. He declined to ride it on the basis that it was a girl's bike (which it was). I reminded him that I was the director and if I wanted him to ride the pink bike then that was the way it was going to have to be. He stared defiantly at me, folded his arms and refused point blank to ride it. Sensing that my negotiating skills were taking a turn for the worse and with little to bargain with, I told him that I would probably feel the same in his position and would therefore turn the bike another colour in post-production. Was there any particular colour that he preferred? We settled on dark blue, sealed the deal with a hi- five, he rode the bike, and thanks to the god of technology we managed to turn it blue in the edit suite a few days later. It was a narrow squeak though, and whenever a filming day with kids looms large I often break out in a cold sweat thinking about it.

HIDDEN CAMERA FILMING

Covert filming of a subject – or any filming of which the subject is unaware – can lead to complications, particularly if you are filming on private property and without permission. Secret filming for the purpose of capturing public responses to humorous situations is one thing, investigative reporting quite another. As to whether you can publish or broadcast your film ultimately depends on whether you have obtained signed permission from those filmed on camera and, if not, whether the content is considered by the legal eagles to be 'in the public's best interest'.

AVOID COPYRIGHT ISSUES

We have already discussed the importance of clearing copyright with regard to archive footage, photographs and music, but it is just as important to avoid any on-screen content that might cause a breach of copyright whilst you are filming out on location. Paintings, drawings, cinema or theatre posters or photographs, indeed any kind of visual branding is fine if it is purely incidental to the scene, but if you make a feature of the work there might be a complaint and you may find you will have to mask a section of your shot in the edit suite.

If you are filming vox pops on the run, just check that logos and posters are not prominently on view behind your subjects and if they are, try to frame them out of shot.

You will also need to obtain releases from anyone you film on camera to avoid the possibility of them asking you to cut their contribution from the final edit, or claiming a percentage of your sales. Misrepresentation of what they said during interview is another possible bone of contention but that is very much your responsibility and we will look at that in more detail in later chapters.

THE IMPORTANCE OF RELEASE FORMS

Releases are not needed if the individual is part of a crowd, in a background shot, or not shown for more than a few seconds or given emphasis within a scene, but if they talk to you or give any kind of a performance, make sure they sign a release form (see Figure 1, pages 90–1). The form does not necessarily need to refer to any payments being made, but there is certainly no harm in

I authorise ANYTIME PRODUCTIONS, currently producing thirteen by twenty-four minute programmes about pot-holing to make use of my interview/appearance in the film *Into the Darkness* (working title).

I agree that you may tape and photograph me, and record my voice, conversation and sounds, including any performance of any musical composition(s) during and in connection with my appearance and hereby give you all consents and assign all rights (including copyright) exclusively to you necessary for the reproduction, exhibition, transmission, broadcast and exploitation thereof or any portion thereof or of a reproduction thereof.

I further agree that you may have the right to use my name, voice, likeness and biographical material concerning me, which I may provide, without time limit, throughout the universe by all means, formats and media (whether now known or hereafter invented) without liability or acknowledgement to me as required under the Copyright, Designs and Patents Act 1988 or otherwise and hereby confirm that all moral rights under this Act or otherwise have been waived.

For the avoidance of doubt, you shall be entitled to cut and edit my interview/appearance as you deem fit and you shall not be obliged to include all or any of the same in any broadcast item.

I further represent that any statements made by me during my appearance are true and that they will not violate or infringe upon the rights of any third party.

Figure 1   Interviewee/appearance release form

For the proper and efficient performance of your services I agree that you will pay me a wholly inclusive fee of £XX. I further acknowledge that you will pay me reasonable travel and subsistence expenses as agreed in connection with this engagement, subject to me submitting full details thereof within fourteen days after such expenditure has been incurred.

It is further acknowledged and agreed that I am self-employed for national insurance and tax purposes and shall be solely responsible for such contributions during the term of this engagement.

Name.................................. ....
(Please print)   (Signature)

Address ....

....

....

Date...................................
Tel No ....

If applicable: I am a parent (or guardian) of the minor who has signed this release and consent and hereby agree that I and the said minor will be bound by all the provisions contained herein.

Name.................................. ....
(Please print)   (Signature)

Date...................................

....
ON BEHALF OF ANYTIME PRODUCTIONS

Figure 1   Interviewee/appearance release form (continued)

inserting a clause which refers to a payment of, say, one pound (unless a formal interview fee has been agreed in advance) being made in return for the interview. This is documentary proof that someone was paid for their services and they agreed to the fee as a buyout without any further payments being due. Release forms can be modified, depending on whether the contributor is, say, a street vox pop, a presenter or an interviewee.

The above example is for signature by a contributor who has travelled to a location to be filmed and with whom you have agreed expenses and an appearance fee. For casual street interviews the references to travel expenses, national insurance and holidays should be omitted from the release form as it is not relevant.

FILMING ON PRIVATE PROPERTY

Whilst you need to be aware of the potential problems filming in public places, the ramifications of filming on private property without permission could also land you in hot water. You do not want to have to abandon a sequence because you were not aware that a particular area was private and it didn't occur to you to check if permission was required. A shopping arcade might seem part of the public domain, for example, but someone will own that property and that someone will almost certainly have security cameras and security officers keeping constant watch. In today's society, CCTV cameras are a part of everyday life and whilst you are busily observing other people, someone may well be observing you – and if they don't like what they see, your filming expedition could be short-lived.

Research your locations thoroughly, check if you need permission to film, agree a location fee in advance if one is required (though it's always worth trying to secure the location for free if possible) and make sure that the owner or proprietor signs a contract. (See Figure 2 on page 94.)

Filming out and about: a matter of common sense

Our streets, our parks and our playgrounds may be part of the public highway but it does not mean you can wander around willy nilly setting up cameras, plugging in cables and generally upsetting the public. Apart from the health and safety aspect of putting people in danger by forcing them to step around cameras into the path of oncoming traffic, there is always the possibility that you will draw unnecessary attention to yourself, even attracting a crowd of onlookers hell bent on making your task as difficult as possible.

Whilst you might find you can walk through towns and cities filming without interruption, it is always advisable to contact the authorities to ensure that you will have a relatively trouble-free shoot. Some parks may request a location fee, and although payment is rarely due for filming on the street – unless you wish to cordon off an area as a public exclusion zone, for which you will need to apply for a permit – the police are generally very co-operative and helpful if they know in advance that you will be out and about on their patch.

I agree that the film/videotape shot on Sunday November 19, 200X at the property named below for an inclusive hire fee of £XXX may be used by ANYTIME PRODUCTIONS and its assigns in part or in whole in such sequence or sequences as they desire. This may be on any copy or format (whether such means, media or formats are now known or hereinafter developed) for their programme provisionally entitled *Into the Darkness* or any programme or publication evolved from it throughout the world in perpetuity.

PROPERTY:
COTTLEY OUTWARD BOUND CENTRE
COTTLEY

....
Signed

....
Date

....
Telephone No

Witnessed by ....

Date ....

Figure 2   Location agreement

9

Plan Ahead

Regardless of the type of film you are making, its subject matter, or its content, you should devise a plan of action so that your time and resources are used effectively. Whether the film is a tightly structured stylised story, or a fly-on-the-wall observation, none of the scenes will fall into place by magic. It is irrelevant, therefore, whether the film is a chronological diary of a soldier's life in Iraq, or a week on the streets with the emergency services, or the trials and tribulations of a rock band on tour, the film will still have a basic set of components – known elements that have numerous possibilities within them – whatever the level of unpredictability within the final narrative.

THINKING AHEAD SAVES TIME AND MONEY

When you start thinking about the components that will eventually comprise your film, you set in motion a chain of events that will ultimately come to fruition in the editing suite. At that point, crucial decisions will need to be made about how the shots and scenes should be juxtaposed for best impact, and how that will affect the balance of the film and its rhythm and tempo. Whilst in some instances such juxtaposition might be left entirely to the creative integrity of the editor who will look at your film with a fresh eye, it is wise to consider all the possibilities at the planning stage. Generating a preconceived vision of the structure will help you formulate your filming needs as you work your way through the pre-production jungle and provide a creative template to help you stay focused.

THOROUGH RESEARCH: AN ESSENTIAL STARTING POINT

If your film is a contemporary drama, your starting point will almost certainly be the creation of a script, followed by decisions about whether it will be studio or location (or both), followed by auditions and casting – all of which we looked at in Chapter 7.

If it is a period drama or drama documentary, it's essential to undertake some detailed research of your facts and check the accuracy of props and wardrobe, because attention to detail will be an important factor in determining whether your film has historical credibility or seen to be full of holes.

If you are making a factual film, you will need to make contact with the people you would like to put on film, and research every aspect of your story in order to make sure you get your facts right, particularly if you are investigating individuals or probing organisations. And try to obtain a balanced viewpoint, offering an opportunity to all contributors to respond to any viewpoints, criticism or accusations.

Areas of research might include:

- the internet
- newspapers and press cuttings
- the library
- specialised journals
- museums

- archive film libraries
- photographic libraries
- video news reports
- experts and specialists
- informed people.

MAKE TIME FOR A RECCE

Whenever it is possible to recce your locations in advance you should arrange to do so as early as possible. A recce will throw up numerous filming possibilities and give you time to resolve any potential problems. It may also strengthen your visualisation of a scene. Standing at a location not only opens your mind to the creative possibilities, it enables you to work out how you might minimise set-ups and maximise shots to save time and avoid moving people and equipment about unnecessarily.

Exploit locations to your advantage

Filming a chase scene with skiers speeding down a mountainside, for example, does not necessarily mean that you have to find a multitude of camera positions from the top of the mountain all the way down to the bottom. By going on a detailed recce you might discover one central position that offers a changing scenario through 360°, allowing you to shoot several set-ups with differing backgrounds, inter-cutting close action ski shots with wider shots, and creating the *illusion* that they are on different parts of the mountain.

As one who has experienced filming such a scenario I can assure you that moving people and equipment around on a giant slab of sloping ice is the kind of stuff of which nightmares are made, and will not turn out to be the quickest, most efficient, or happiest experience of your life unless you can exploit the situation to best advantage.

Run scenes in your head

And remember to run your 'completed' film, or particular scenes, in your head if you can, so that you can turn that vision into practical application. Claudio von Planta, you will recall, was able to film an entire action scene for *Long Way Round* because he visualised how his shots could be juxtaposed into a strong narrative in the edit suite. Although the events unfolded before him in real time and he had to react spontaneously, on a recce he might have envisaged the same scene (because the road was impassable and therefore the scenario inevitable), but possibly been able to consider some additional shots by factoring them into his thinking, and ultimately the schedule.

TAKE CONTROL WHENEVER YOU CAN

Although documentary filming can be largely unpredictable, you should take control of situations and set-ups wherever possible to avoid dealing with unnecessary complications on the filming day – not least of which is the possibility of over-shooting and the ramifications of that on the edit. Control does not mean stage-managing scenarios but implementing damage limitation and positive solutions with regard to the practical aspects of capturing your story on film. I offer you two examples to clarify this.

Control at a venue

You want to make a film about a Welsh choir singing in a concert hall, or a band performing on a stage. You may not know exactly what will happen on the night, but three important questions should immediately spring to mind:

- What are the dates and times of the rehearsals and performances?
- How do I cover them effectively with camera and sound?
- Are there any restrictions on where I can operate from within the venue?

It is unlikely that anyone giving a performance will turn up on the day, plug in their instruments and fill the air with wondrous, captivating music without first having a rehearsal. Apart from the fact that the rehearsal would be a useful scene to have in the film, it gives you a chance to assess sound and stage lighting levels, think about camera positions, and become familiar with the songs that will be performed and the order they will be performed in.

You can then work out how these might be best covered in terms of close shots, mid shots and wide shots – and if you decide you might want coverage of the audience as well, you will almost certainly need to factor in two, if not three, cameras. You would also be advised to work closely with the technical crew who organise the stage sound and lighting so that there is no conflict of interest, the crew hopefully offering to supply you with a sound output from their own mixing desk. And make your own technical needs very clear to them as there will be little or no time just prior to the performance to correct any misunderstandings.

And if you decide to record interviews during breaks in rehearsals, take the opportunity at the recce to look for suitable dressing rooms that might have interesting backgrounds, or ground level shots, or even high angles from balconies that might offer an interesting backdrop, away from any high levels of activity or noise.

Control on the streets

A street carnival in any town or city in any part of the world offers all kinds of exciting possibilities, but the dream scenario of spectacle, colour, music, dance and visual vibrancy might court disaster if you do not plan the shoot in advance. Knowing the route that the procession will take is a positive starting point. Advance knowledge of the order of the various floats and marching bands will give you a chance to decide an order of priority for filming, and details of any roads that will be closed on the day will help with the scheduling of the movement of cameras and equipment. Making contact with the local authority, the police and the carnival organisers would also go a long way to smoothing your filming day.

Again, two or more cameras might be needed to do full justice to the story, and, as before, you should consider possible interview backdrops and the best way to avoid any problems with noise and crowd interference.

Filming 'everything that moves' may turn out to be your only option because of the nature of the story, but by considering different camera angles and possible cutaways on the recce, you might save yourself a lot of head-banging when it comes to piecing the jigsaw puzzle together later.

You should also seek technical advice about how to keep pictures and sound synchronous in the event of employing two or more cameras that are not cabled and controlled through a portable vision mixer. You will need to make sure that your edit facility can run multiple picture rushes in synch with the sound, allowing full control over the edit points.

Forewarned is forearmed

Assuming you are not self-shooting or multi-tasking the entire project by yourself, but collaborating with others (a very wise step), a recce will provide advanced intelligence that will be of benefit to *everyone* involved in the making of your film, because nobody wants to turn up on a shoot and find too many surprises being thrown at them – especially the kind that should have been flagged up and addressed beforehand.

When you film on location there are four main enemies lying in wait to ambush you:

- the weather
- time
- noise
- practical difficulties.

Knowing that a million permutations of setback possibilities could emanate from these basic problem zones, you should take the necessary steps to contain them as much as possible, long before you turn up with cameras, lights, generators, props, crew and actors.

There is very little we can do about the weather, except drag out our prayer mats and hope for the best, but checking on a long-range weather forecast will certainly give you some indication of your prospects, possibly allowing you to schedule the morning and afternoon segments accordingly. In the summer, longer days will give you a fighting chance to complete on time, but in winter be wary of underestimating your shooting schedule, since substituting God's light for artificial light at the end of the filming day can create horrendous continuity problems.

Time, of course, is the greatest enemy of the film-maker, as it will start running out on you faster than you could ever imagine – so the more you plan, the better your chances of success.

TAKE PRACTICAL STEPS TO AVOID LOCATION PROBLEMS

In any scenario, taking the following practical steps can eliminate most potential problems and obstacles:

- Take digital photographs for later reference.
- Sketch out ground plans, including possible camera positions.
- Look for high buildings or accessible vantage points for high angles.
- Assess areas where the movement of equipment may be limited.
- Mark the position of the sun and the time of day on a rough location map.
- Assess whether anything is likely to change between the recce and the shoot.
- Obtain permission to film from land and property owners.
- Agree any location or facility fees in advance.
- Check out potential noise issues.
- Check for power points or a power supply.
- Decide if you will need any communications equipment.
- Check that there is adequate parking.
- Check for the nearest café, toilets, hotel and hospital.
- Purchase local maps of the area.
- Assess safety issues and any potential hazards.

Reference photographs are a must

As a starting point, I would recommend the purchase of a digital camera to take with you on your recce. It does not have to be a high-end, all-singing, all-dancing, super deluxe Nikon or Pentax. Any digital camera will do, as long as it has a memory card with ample storage, and you can review your pictures as you go.

It's surprising how much you can forget about a location from the time you recce to the time you sit down and draw up a shooting schedule. Not only will recce photographs give you an exact visual representation of the location site, but you can use them to draw up rough floor plans to plot your camera positions and, if you are not self-shooting, to show your camera operator and sound recordist.

In some instances, you may need others who are involved in the film to see the photographs: a designer trying to match a physical background with props, perhaps, or a facilities house supplying tracking equipment to be used over rough terrain. If any production personnel who need to be involved live some distance away, or are currently travelling abroad, you can copy the photos to your computer and send them as email attachments for their immediate assessment and response.

Assess your camera positions

There is nothing more likely to cost you valuable time than turning up at a shoot and standing around scratching your head as you decide where the cameras should be placed. Even straightforward establishing shots or interviews need thinking about, and if you have checked out your shots on the recce, camera and sound can be set up immediately. Better still, if you managed to mark them on a rough floor plan, everyone involved in the shoot can see immediately what the gameplan is and react accordingly. Wherever possible, consider tracking the camera – it can make your shots much more interesting and varied as foreground and background imagery combine to create a more three-dimensional look.

Not all of your scenes necessarily need to be shot at ground level. If you want high angles, for instance, it would be wise to check out the possibilities in advance. High-rise flats and car parks offer natural panoramic vistas, but you may need permission to film from them. Hillsides and cliff tops are another possibility – but are there any access problems? Will it take too long to move the equipment? A recce for your street carnival, for example, gives you the opportunity to line up possible shots from street positions, and to investigate any high vantage points along the route that would be advantageous in showing the full splendour of the event.

Reference photographs of the carnival would show the width of pavements and streets, with possible accessibility for a motorcycle or car for obtaining tracking shots, whilst town maps clearly marked up would show where streets will be closed on the day and the traffic re-routed. Pictures for the venue of a rock concert would reveal seating configurations for audience cutaways; show aisles and fire exits that you should not block, possible positions on the stage for a remote, hand-held camera, and general positions for fixed cameras and any additional lighting.

Never take situations for granted

Even if everything seems to be controllable, you can often come unstuck because you did not think everything through properly. You might want to film two simple scenes at a school, for example, one in a classroom, one in a playground. But if you didn't check pupil break times, you might suddenly find yourself ambushed by a mob of screaming schoolchildren who bring the filming session to an abrupt, albeit temporary, end. And if you move from the playground to the classroom only to find it locked because you didn't organise entry, everyone has to stand around waiting for a key to be located before you can be let in.

Beware of changing scenarios

What you find on the recce day isn't always what you will find on the shoot. A school inspection, or fire drills, or corridors closed for cleaning or renovation might mean taking long detours from one place to another. A field that is completely accessible might, in just a few days of rain, turn itself into a boggy marsh, with a dry river bed transformed into a fast-flowing stream some two feet deep, with you and your crew ill-equipped to cross it because you didn't bring waders or planks to form a bridge.

And always mark the position of the sun on a rough floor plan, or map, along with the time of day. Few shots favour the sun glinting directly into the lens or creating heavy shadows where you don't want them, so knowing the sun's likely position at any time of day could affect the scheduling of your shots and save you a lot of time and frustration. You may also need to determine if any breaks in filming – in particular, coffee or lunch, or setting up for reverse angles – might affect continuity because of changing lighting conditions, in which case a rethink of the schedule would prove advantageous.

Agree a location fee in advance

You should agree a plan of action and a location fee with any private landowners or property owners at the recce if at all possible, and make sure a written agreement or contract is signed on the spot, or very soon afterwards. Those not familiar with the weird and wonderful ways of the film-making fraternity may not fully appreciate the ramifications of allowing cameras on their property, so you have to make it very clear what your intentions are. You do not want to spend time arguing with landlords or business proprietors on a shoot day because of any misunderstandings about numbers of people, the amount of equipment, the upheaval being caused – followed by a demand for a renegotiation of the fee.

Check out potential noise problems

You should take the opportunity to assess noise levels from roads, schools, trains and airfields. Never assume that because it is quiet during the recce that peace and tranquillity will favour you when the cameras start to roll.

- If there is a local school near to the location, check the school term times.
- If there is a railway station nearby, check the train times and pick up a timetable.
- Check if any local road repairs or building works are scheduled.
- Look for streams and babbling brooks that may turn into noisy, fast-flowing rivers after a period of heavy rain.
- Check for areas where the public might suddenly converge on the filming day: camp and picnic sites, for instance, or a nearby moto cross, racing circuit, air show or rock concert.

Establish if there is a power supply

Filming away from a studio means you may need to power lights, especially for interior scenes, so check with the owner, proprietor, or house electrician, that there are ample electrical sockets and enough power to service your needs. If not, you will need to organise a generator to take to the location. Even if your original plan involved filming outside scenes using natural light, things may change on the day if the weather becomes overcast, or you are forced to film inside for whatever reason.

Formulate a checklist

To ensure that nothing is overlooked it is always a good idea to draw up a location checklist, so that comments and contact details can be scribbled down at the recce whilst they are fresh in your mind. A priority would be a number and address for the local hospital. Whilst you can always summon help through 999, on occasions it may be more appropriate, and quicker, to transport any injured personnel directly to the hospital rather than wait for an ambulance, if you are sure they can be moved.

Finding a contact for a local dentist would also be useful if your shoot is going to be scheduled over several weeks.

You will also need to make sure that there will be adequate parking at the location for everyone involved in the shoot, and if not, what the alternative arrangements would be.

And there are many other things that can easily be overlooked but are just as important: the nearest café or restaurant for lunch and supper breaks; toilets; the nearest boarding house or hotel, not just for making advanced bookings but also if there is a last minute change of plan and you, or members of the unit, have to stay over.

BE PREPARED WHEN FILMING ABROAD

If your film – or any part of your film – is to be shot abroad, additional requirements will need to be considered, because filming in a foreign country is never straightforward. This is hardly surprising when you consider the potential for misinterpretation and confusion, for example:

- communications problems, most notably language
- geographical problems
- time differences
- cultural differences
- misunderstandings of local laws and customs
- arrangements of local fixers and interpreters
- possible visa requirements
- equipment carnet requirements
- awareness of no-go areas.

Plan your trip well in advance

Before you even set off on your journey into the great unknown you will need to make advanced arrangements in order to smooth your passage and that of anyone accompanying you. Flying out to a war zone or an area of civil unrest, or a country about to be engulfed in a hurricane or a military coup would, not surprisingly, be most unwise (unless of course your film is about hurricanes and military coups). If you don't have the benefit of access to the BBC's regularly updated list of places-to-think-carefully-about-before-visiting, you should check with your travel agent or a particular country's local Embassy to assess if it is a likely trouble spot, and to verify if you will need a visa.

If you plan to travel abroad you must hold a full ten-year passport, even for a day trip. Some countries have an immigration requirement for a passport to remain valid for a minimum period (usually at least six months) beyond the date of entry to that country.

Make sure your passport is in good condition and valid for at least six months at the date of your return. This is a requirement of the country you are travelling to, not the passport office. Any questions should again be addressed to the British Embassy or the Consulate or Embassy of the country you wish to travel to.

You should also check if you need any vaccinations or special documents that will allow you access to places off the beaten track, particularly if the public are not usually authorized to be there. And don't forget those small items that suddenly become of major importance, such as diarrhoea tablets, mosquito spray and sun cream.

Find help when filming in unfamiliar surroundings

Stepping off a plane, boat or train in a foreign land can be an unnerving experience if you are not prepared. An awareness of the driving laws is always a good start, with air conditioning essential inside any hire vehicle you plan to use in a warm country. Maps of the area are indispensable if you plan to travel without a local guide, but whenever possible you should arrange, in advance, for the services of a fixer who speaks your language as well as the local languages, and who can translate and sort out problems as and when they arise, particularly when dealing with the authorities.

Take time to adjust to new surroundings

You should allow time to acclimatise before racing off to get things done. Jet lag can be positively dangerous if you are too tired to concentrate properly, especially if you go jumping into a vehicle, ready to hit the road. Unfamiliar temperatures can further add to your discomfort, and diverse cultures, customs and attitudes could delay you indefinitely if you are not fully prepared for all eventualities.

As soon as you are on foreign soil my advice would be to take 24 hours to chill out and sit down with everyone involved to work out a plan of action. Organising a foreign recce and shoot by yourself is really not advisable, so a worthy investment would be the hire of a freelance production manager, or production co-ordinator, to make all the necessary arrangements in advance of your trip.

Arrange a carnet as soon as possible

The production manager can also arrange insurance on your equipment, and a carnet, which you will need for filming in most countries worldwide, including the US, Canada, Australia, most of Asia and South Africa. As a British citizen you will not need a carnet for filming in any European Union country, but you should carry an equipment list with you, detailing serial numbers and proof of purchase or hire. The carnet is an international customs document that permits the duty-free temporary import of your equipment. By presenting a carnet to foreign customs officials, you pass duty free and tax free into that country, bypassing the time-consuming business of completing numerous customs documents for each individual country you are visiting. The carnet also provides a financial guarantee to foreign customs officials that, in the event that the goods, which have been temporarily admitted to a country, are not re-exported, import duties and taxes will be paid. There are companies that will organise carnets for a fee, based on the country you are travelling to and how soon you will need it.

Once you have the carnet in your possession it is vital you get it stamped and signed every time you enter or leave a country. You do not want to find yourself in a foreign land, unable to speak the language, and showing every single item on your equipment list to a customs officer – then possibly paying a huge fine. No, seriously, you don't.

You should also make early contact with a facilities company in the country you are visiting. It is often easier, and sometimes more cost effective, to hire your equipment abroad, or certain items of equipment, such as lights, rather than carry them around with you everywhere.

In any event, knowing where to hire a back-up camera in an emergency might just come in handy when you are most in need of an olive branch. Getting any kind of professional help for a foreign shoot, in fact, will ultimately save you time, money and a million unnecessary headaches.

HEALTH AND SAFETY A PRIORITY

There is only one thing more important than you and your production unit making your film successfully – and that's making your film *safely*.

Putting people at risk during the production is both irresponsible and unnecessary, and can be avoided if you follow some basic guidelines, much of which comes down to common sense. It is a legal requirement for all producers employed in broadcast companies to submit a risk assessment form to the health and safety officer and all production personnel, but even if yours is a small, low-budget movie using friends and relatives, it would be wise to assess any safety hazards in order to avoid the possibility of accidents for which you could be held personally responsible.

There are more health and safety risks on a film shoot than you would think possible. For a start, people working excessively long hours, sometimes without proper breaks, can lead to fatigue, loss of concentration, and ultimately accidents.

Physical hazards – the lifting and moving of heavy props, sets, camera equipment and lights – account for a high proportion of accidents, as do falls from heights and electricity related incidents. Then there are environmental risks, such as noise, temperature and water, the use of hazardous substances such as chemicals, and the preparation of food.

The last thing you need on your production is to be sued for negligence if an accident occurs, so you would be strongly advised to identify any potential health and safety hazards on your recce and bring them to the attention of everyone who will be involved in the production. If you are filming on someone else's premises – a busy factory, a boat-building yard, a theme park – you will be required to follow the company's health and safety guidelines as a condition of being on site, and a representative may insist on accompanying you at all times.

Ensure that everyone is aware of the risks

If children are involved in your shoot it is a legal requirement to submit a Young Person's Risk Assessment form, obtainable from the local authority, and if you are making your film for an independent film company or a broadcaster you should apply to them for the documentation. Each company's risk assessment forms differ slightly and will list the company's Codes of Practice on the hazard checklist. And even if your film is a low-budget production being made by you and a few friends, you should create your own risk assessment form to take with you on your recce so that everyone can be made aware of the potential hazards. (See Figure 3, pages 114–15.)

There are many people around you who could be at risk whilst you are filming:

- the production crew
- members of the public
- performers, presenters and actors
- business and corporation employees
- property owners.

To give you an indication of the safety hazards that can lie in wait, the document on pages 114–15 is a mock-up of a typical risk assessment form.

Take action to eliminate risk

Having identified who is most likely to be at risk in any situation, you should then consider what action needs to be taken, either in advance of filming or during filming, in a control priority:

- eliminate
- substitute
- isolate
- supervise
- have experienced staff and specialists in attendance
- distribute protective clothing and safety equipment.

ANYTIME PRODUCTIONS
Risk Assessment

Title of production:
Anytime Productions contact number:
Description of shoot:
Production date:
Location address:
Producer:

Specialist contractors:
Equipment hire:

Emergency Arrangements and First Aid Requirements

Nearest Accident and Emergency:
First Aider at the location:

Distribution List (tick to confirm the document has been forwarded)

Producer		Artistes or presenters in vision	
Director		Make-up	
Set designer		Cameraman	
Health and safety officer		Sound recordist	
Films operation manager		Electrician	

Figure 3   Risk assessment form

Possible Risks

Use the checklist below to identify hazards or risks on your shoot that are applicable to the listed activity. Please tick the appropriate box.

No.	Hazard or risk		No.	Hazard or risk	
1	Access difficulties		25	Manual handling	
2	Alcohol/hospitality		26	Night operations	
3	Animals		27	Noise	
4	Artist using special props or tools		28	Portable tools above 110V	
5	Special needs: e.g. elderly, the disabled, deaf, blind		29	Derelict buildings: e.g. rats, asbestos, gases, dangerous structures	
6	Compressed gas, cryogenics		30	Radiation	
7	Confined spaces: e.g. lifts, mines, sewers, tanks, restricted sets		31	Risk of infection	
8	Crowds/public/civil unrest/streets/parks		32	Design and construction of sets, construction materials	
9	Scaffolds, rostra, working platforms, practical staircases		33	Scenery hazards: e.g. stage revolves, deceptive shapes and moves, non-fire retardant	
10	Camera operations: cranes, cables, remote, steadicam		34	Scene dock storage	
11	Prop hazards: e.g. practical, glass, non-fire retardant, water		35	Smoking	
12	Working at heights		36	Fire procedures and exposed flame	
13	Electricity, electrical appliances		37	Special visual effects	
14	Excavation		38	Sports events	
15	Explosives/pyrotechnics/fireworks		39	Stunts	
16	Fatigue/long hours/physical exertion/stress		40	Extremes of temperature and temperature changes	
17	Lifting equipment: e.g. fork lift trucks, cranes		41	Vehicles/motorcycles, filming from, artists driving	
18	Flammable materials and liquids: LPG, bottled gases, petrol, paints and sprays		42	Water: working in or near, use of tanks/boats/diving into	
19	Weapons		43	Children and young persons	
20	Food preparation		44	Flying: aircraft, balloons, parachutes, hang-gliders	
21	Grid contractors		45	Working abroad	
22	Hazardous substances: dusts, vapours, fume, oils, mists, acids		46	Extremes of weather	
23	Lasers and stroboscopic effects		47	Possible violence	
24	Audiences and stewarding		48	Other	

Figure 3   Risk assessment form (continued)

You should list all relevant preventative actions you plan to take on a separate sheet and attach it to the Risk Assessment for distribution.

Typical preventative scenarios

Item 10 lists camera operations, an obvious necessity for a film shoot, but your typed-up checklist should indicate what measures will be taken to ensure that everyone will be able to work safely. Declaring that an experienced crew will supervise equipment at all times is a commitment that you should make sure is enforced, with a proviso to everyone present that they should follow instructions from the cameraman and electrician, and not enter filming areas unless given permission.

Item 25 lists manual handling, which again is obvious in an environment where so much equipment is constantly being moved about. But if there is heavy furniture involved, for instance, you should indicate that arrangements have been made so that only the design department, and possibly experienced furniture removers, will perform any manual handling necessary.

It is obviously a bonus if you can have an experienced First Aider or nurse on your shoot, but for all the benefits they bring, prevention is always better than cure.

10

The Creative Framework

Once you have completed the research and recce you need to sit down and think carefully about your creative approach. If you are filming a documentary it is unlikely that you will produce an actual script – unless there are stylised inserts or drama segments – but you should put something *down on paper as a point of focus. And if it's a fictional film, you'll need to have a completed script and find a group of suitable actors to audition before you can start the production ball rolling.*

DECIDING ON THE FILMIC STYLE

There is a possibility that nothing you discovered in the research and recce phase has affected your original creative concept, but various factors may have come to light that require an adjustment in your thinking; a key contributor who has decided not to participate, perhaps, or the loss of a location that will change the visual look of the film.

Assuming the basic spine of your story has remained intact, your research should have helped you develop the idea further and given you the opportunity to evaluate all of the possibilities. Deciding on a filmic style should be reasonably straightforward if, indeed, it has changed at all. What, or who, will drive the narrative? Will the story be humorous, satirical, investigative? Will you use one basic style or several? Will it be artistic or commercial?

DETERMINING A RUNNING TIME

In my experience, short films can run anything up to ten minutes before they risk over-reaching themselves. If you have decided to make a film for a specific broadcast slot, say *Three Minute Wonder* or *Four Docs*, or for a particular film festival, then your final running time will be more specifically established.

If not, you need to gauge carefully the value of your content against its running time, and how you intend to market the end product. If the purpose of your film is simply to showcase your talents or to make a submission as a pilot idea, you need to ensure that every frame of every shot will hold its audience from start to finish. Making a three-minute film that does not do justice to its subject matter, or a twelve-minute film that looks and feels like it has outstayed its welcome are among the biggest mistakes a first time film-maker can make. A story that fits snugly into its running time reveals a director who has control over the content and its entertainment value for the audience.

One factor might be the amount of time or money you have at your disposal to make your film, especially if actors, technicians, equipment and locations have to be paid for. Another could be the complexity of the story itself, particularly if you are using dramatic recreations and eye-witness accounts to build tension. Your film may, on the other hand, be purely observational, a simple narrative driven by sound effects, natural dialogue and music, and, as such, a snapshot of an event rather than a detailed filmic journey.

Be realistic about what you can achieve

Whatever the nature of the story, the golden rule is not to be over ambitious and to be realistic about what you can achieve, based on the merit and possible limitations of the content. To make it compelling and meaningful every scene needs to take the story forward without treading water, be full of interesting information and visual interpretation, and a joy to watch. Some of the most effective short films I have seen in recent years encapsulate excitement and emotion inside eight minutes without the viewer feeling either short-changed or restless. And there's always the possibility that you can re-edit your film to a shorter time length for particular broadcast time slots or festivals.

TRANSLATING THE CREATIVE CONCEPT INTO A PRACTICAL REALITY

Having decided on the overall style and technique, you need to translate your creative idea into a practical reality. When you analyse your components list you may find that accessibility or cost may now mean you have to tailor or trim your initial ambitions, though you obviously still want to make your film with the least amount of compromise. Apart from the interviewee who has suddenly got cold feet and the beautiful location that turned into a traveller's encampment overnight, you discover that the vital piece of archive footage you wanted so badly will now cost you three arms and a leg, and has to be replaced with something else. Are these bad omens? Not in the slightest. Experienced film-makers never expect things to run smoothly, so why should you?

Being adaptable is part of the film-maker's armoury; the protective shield that shuns impossibility and defeat and looks for a challenge in every disappointment – because nothing is going to stand in the way of you making your film. And anyway, it's not all bad news. An unexpected eye witness you came across will definitely add another dimension to your story, a spectacular new location will give you some truly inspiring backdrops, and a man you met in a pub showed you, quite by chance, some old photographs and a home movie that will provide a level of information and emotion that you could have only dared dream of.

So, you work out your master plan, knowing that things will change in the telling, but looking to make the most out of every new discovery so that the blueprint does not become the be-all and end-all, but a way forward and part of the great adventure.

FOCUSING ON CREATING A STRONG NARRATIVE

But don't start budgeting yet. Films are not made by the director constantly working out content values on screen against the cost factor, or what percentages should be used of interviews against action scenes or archive footage. Like all creative processes, a film is an evolving process, its content shifting and changing with each new filming day and each new edit, until the desired shape and balance is achieved. Until you are sure what is important to the telling of your story and what is not, you should allow your mind to be free from the burden of finance and scheduling (apart from discoveries that have already put certain items out of reach and have therefore been eliminated), so that you can focus on moulding the strongest possible narrative from your story components.

Explore the creative possibilities

Experience teaches many of us that an unfolding chain of events captured on camera does not mean that you necessarily have to limit your creative control over those events. There are many films, of course, that tell an honest story in a straightforward way, without any frills, and devoid of stylisation or creative flair; their subject matter not benefiting from strong visualisations or emotive music. Investigative films often probe the seamier side of life, dealing with people and situations that shock and appal us, and there is little the film-maker can do, or even want to do, other than use their integrity to tell it as it is. There is a place for every kind of film-maker and every kind of genre – but if you want your film to stand out from the crowd you should consider how it might combine imagination and innovation in the strongest possible way.

If you are planning to submit a proposal for your film to a studio or a broadcaster you will ultimately have to produce a shooting schedule and a budget for them to look over, but first and foremost any potential backers or producers will want to see an outline of your idea – a treatment – so that they can gauge its suitability and whether it has conceptual merit.

Writing up a treatment will strengthen the vision

Even if you are not submitting a treatment to a broadcaster it is often a good idea to write down an outline of your story idea, not only so that you can see the idea taking shape on the page, but because everyone who will be involved in the project can share your initial vision and help you develop it.

Figure 4 (pages 122–3) is a treatment for an entertainment documentary on the history of magic called *Smoke and Mirrors*. The opening paragraph is written with the specific intention of engaging the reader immediately, the subsequent paragraphs giving an overview of the content and the way that content will be creatively handled. It has been developed from a short film made previously about the life of one of the featured magicians.

Smoke and Mirrors

A Treatment

Roll up! Roll up! Watch in amazement as the Master Magician drives giant spikes through his voluptuous assistant! Wait with baited breath as the Chinese Conjuror catches a fiery bullet between his teeth! Avert your gaze as the fiendish Wizard dissects a member of the audience into several pieces!

These were just some of the acts that drew millions to the theatre in the late 1800s. Audiences were mesmerised by feats of transformation, levitation, escapology, mind-reading and illusion that were paraded before them. By the turn of the century over 4,000 magicians of all nationalities were playing on variety bills across the world, and head and shoulders above it all stood some of the most flamboyant and inventive performers in the history of entertainment.

Smoke and Mirrors is proposed as a one-hour documentary adopting a powerful and imaginative visual style in keeping with both the subject matter and audience's expectations of the magic of television in the twenty-first century. Each show will assume a central theme within which any number of elements can be featured, whether personal recollections and insights, stage recreations, rostrum photographs or archive footage. The individual shows, whilst being part of a central style, would offer thematic variety relevant to the subject, be that Oriental, Americana, English Music Hall, or dark, mysterious and gothic.

Figure 4   A treatment for *Smoke and Mirrors*

The overall look, therefore, would be innovative and stylised. Where no footage exists of performances by the great magicians, recreations would be filmed, with diffused imagery, often soft-focused to reflect an abstract timelessness, with cutaways of audiences in period costume treated in the same filmic manner. Low-key imagery and strong backlighting would also maintain a sense of mystery, suspense and drama within these segments. *Smoke and Mirrors* will contrast the old and the new in a stunning presentation that is unique and fresh.

Theatre programmes, press clippings and billboards would frequently contain recreated moving imagery or archive footage in place of photographs, sometimes with a visual treatment to give a sense of wonder and fantasy. There is a wealth of documented material and memorabilia at the Magic Circle Museum in London and at the Society of American Magicians, hundreds of detailed books on the craft and history of magic, and many hours of film footage dating from 1896, along with television footage of all the great contemporary magicians, including Channing Pollock, Doug Henning, Robert Harbin and David Copperfield.

The lives of these exceptional men and women are a lasting testament to integrity, resourcefulness and ingenuity at the highest level and are the ingredients, we believe, for a truly inspirational and magical series.

Figure 4 A treatment for *Smoke and Mirrors* (continued)

Enthusing people to your project is important, because if you can excite and interest them at an early stage, the chances are that it will only get better in the telling – and writing up a treatment gives you a very positive point of focus.

FORMULATING A CREATIVE TEMPLATE

In previous chapters we have looked at the various approaches and styles you might take with your film. A drama script will fire up the imagination, its visual treatment clear for all to see, regardless of whether it comprises traditional narrative, flashbacks, flash forwards, fantasy sequences or abstract and surreal imagery.

A documentary is not so easy to visualise due to the shifting nature of its content and its unpredictability. This does not mean, however, that you cannot have a vision. You could, of course, shoot your film chronologically, as events unfold, and edit them together with the minimum of juxtaposition – but risk creating a dull and uninspiring movie. If you want to engage your audience and put your own individual stamp as a film-maker on it, you will need to work at it, applying some creative and structural thinking in pre-production as well as during filming and at the edit.

Assess the story elements

The research and recce would already have put much of the content of your film into perspective, and a structure may have begun forming in your mind. Meeting and talking with your contributors and interviewees would have provided vital information that will not only take the story forward but move it in various directions. And since all the material – your story components – supporting the main dialogue sections will have been assimilated, this just leaves you with the job of deciding how all these elements might be blended together into a cohesive and compelling structure.

You could assemble all the rushes in the edit suite and make a structural decision at that point, but the editor would still like to see a gameplan, no matter how rough. Even if you are editing the material yourself, you really want to avoid being overwhelmed by several hours' worth of footage and not quite knowing where to begin.

Clarify your story spine

Another possibility to consider then, is devising a creative template prior to the shoot. If you propose to add any stylisation to your film – dramatic recreations, fantasy elements, prose and poetry readings, musical visualisations – they will all need to have some contextual meaning and progression within the story, so it would be of enormous benefit to map them out well before filming begins.

Devising a creative template does not mean that you are proposing to manipulate the people and events in your film. Providing that your film reflects both the incidents and the experiences of its participants accurately, and without distortion, you are merely hanging some visual creative devices onto a central story spine.

Remember Simon Chambers' fictional diary to his grandmother informing her of his discoveries whilst he investigated the activities of Rio Tinto. Or the abstract imagery and email device used in *The Mythologist* to try and track down the elusive Armen Victorian. Or the visual interpretation of the number three in *The Secret*, the story of Arthur, trapped forever by his Obsessive Compulsive Disorder.

There is no misrepresentation of the facts within these stories, and although *The Company We Keep* follows Simon Chambers' investigation of Rio Tinto chronologically, its innovative approach makes it all the more appealing and watchable.

Devising a creative template opens your mind to the possibilities within your film, helping you to structure and shape it accordingly. This framework might change by varying degrees during the actual filming, but creating one can concentrate your imagination on all kinds of options and opportunities you might not have previously considered; a vision of how the finished film might look; a guide to carry with you throughout the production for reference and ongoing development.

The creative template as a working model

Let's look at the hypothetical real life story of a woman suffering from bad dreams, which we'll call *Dream World*. Maybe you chanced across the story in a local paper, or it cropped up in conversation with the woman herself at a social gathering. You are intrigued by the story. You ask her if she would mind talking to you about it on film, then you write up a treatment.

Converting an idea into a creative template

Let us assume that the treatment for *Dream World* has been based on careful research; talking to the woman at home, and her sister on the telephone, discussing the problem with a specialist and various psychologists, people you have been introduced to who are also sufferers, and by reading various reports about the effect of dreams on humans generally.

Dream World
A Treatment

Imagine living vast moments of your life as a waking dream, not able to discern what is real and what is not. Imagine the trepidation every time you climb into bed, not knowing what horrifying journeys you will embark on as the endless darkness transforms into daylight hours that still bring no relief from the torments inside your mind. Then imagine walking down the street, or driving your car, as a feeling of nausea overtakes you and, for several terrifying moments, you believe you are still sleeping and the real world has drifted once again into horrifying fantasy.

For Dawn Taylor this is no fantasy. Ever since she had seen her sister Claire's car crash in a dream three months before the accident occurred, dreams have dominated her life. Hardly daring to go to bed or even leave the house, her mind has been taken hostage and she can find no way to escape. In an attempt to resolve the crisis, Dawn has decided to seek help from a sleep psychiatrist in Scotland. Dr Sean Myers has a reputation for analysing dreams and sleep patterns, and has promised to do what he can to help her.

Dawn's story will be in the form of a quest; the journey of a woman suffering from terminal exhaustion; a desperate woman at the end

Figure 5   A treatment for *Dream World*

of her tether. The film opens with a recreation of her sister's car crash, with Dawn's recollections of the incident in voice-over. The main narrative drive will be Dawn herself, talking to us about her dreams and their implications on her life, and Dr Myers on how dreams can affect us generally and about Dawn's condition specifically.

Although *Dream World* is a serious factual story, it will adopt a stylistic approach in the illustration of the dreams whilst using more conventional techniques to portray the heart-rending experiences of a woman coming face to face with her demons. The trip to Scotland, though real, will have an abstract quality, giving us cause to question whether even this journey itself is real or imaginary, and other sufferers' dreams will be illustrated as surreal recreations to show the true horror of what they are going through. We shall delve into Dawn's childhood, revealing a disagreement with her parents that kept them apart for many years, and her desire to be an artist that was never fulfilled.

The quest concludes as Dawn confronts her own fears and relates her experiences to Dr Myers in an emotional session as he endeavours to get to the truth. Are we, the audience, about to discover for ourselves what is real and what is imaginary?

Figure 5   A treatment for *Dream World* (continued)

Based on your research, you have decided to adopt a stylised approach; a montage of dream-like imagery in keeping with the spine of the story itself and reinforcing the horrors and devastating effect they have on the sufferers. Although these images will be manufactured, they are based on imagery that is very real to the victims, and since these dreams only exist in people's minds, this may well be the best way to illustrate them.

Before devising a creative template for your film (see Figure 6 on pages 130–1), however, it would be an idea to list the story components as a starting point for mapping out a possible structure:

- interviews on camera: Dawn, Claire, Dr Myers
- other sufferers' interviews
- shots of Dawn asleep in bed and walking her local streets
- Dawn's journey from Manchester to Stirling
- establishers of the Scottish Highlands and Dr Myers at work
- photos or home movies from Dawn or Claire's personal collections
- recreation of the car crash
- recreations of Dawn's dreams
- recreations of other sufferers' dreams.

In this particular story you will ultimately discover a great deal of exposition and a strong subtext due to a strained relationship between Dawn and Claire that you are unaware of until you are in the middle of filming. Although you do not know every aspect of the story yet, you can devise your template on what you *do* know, accepting that although the template may change, it offers you a point of focus as you develop it throughout the various production stages. It is not a script but an overview of the sequence possibilities.

ACTION	SOUND
Visual recreation of Claire's car crash	Eerie music. Dawn's voice-track relates the horror of the dream.
Dawn's interview in vision	Dawn reveals how the crash was a catalyst for many that followed.
Visual recreation of one of Dawn's dreams	Dawn voice-over (v/o) describes a typical dream.
Dawn interview intercut with: Dawn asleep in bed Dawn walking the streets	Dawn tells us how the dreams have affected her daily life, that she often never knows if she is awake or in a dream, and that she has decided to seek help.
Scottish Highlands establishers Dr Myers at work	Dr Myers explains the impact on dreams for many people and the different degrees by which they suffer.
Interviews with various dream sufferers	Comments and descriptions of typical bad dreams.
Surreal, recreations of sufferers' dreams	Surrealist music and v/o comments from Dr Myers and sufferers.
Dawn sets off in her car	Lyrical music, possibly guitar. Dawn tells us of her hopes to be able to cure the problem.

Figure 6   Sample of a creative template

Abstract imagery as if the journey to Scotland is part of a dream (car vanishing, reappearing, river background changing to forest etc)	Dr Myers explains some of the methods he will use to try to help Dawn.
Interview with Claire intercut with: Family photographs and home movie clips	Claire tells us how Dawn had a normal childhood, with no advance warning of the problems to come.
More abstract scenes of Dawn's journey to the Highlands	Dawn tells us of the rift with her parents, which she regrets, and of her apprehension in going to Scotland. Will the dreams eventually vanish or get worse? How confident is she of a solution?
Dawn arrives in Scotland and meets Dr Myers	Natural sound of the first meeting between Dawn and Dr Myers.
Interview Dr Myers	Myers tells us of his first impressions on meeting Dawn.
Dr Myers starts work on helping Dawn	Dawn v/o summarises her desperate need to be free of the torment.
Surreal imagery of Dawn's dreams intercut with Dr Myers in consultation with Dawn	Will we finally discover what is real and what is imaginary in Dawn's life?

Figure 6   Sample of a creative template (continued)

Allow your template to be flexible

Creating a table divided into story segments in this way – with action on the left and sound on the right – gives you an at-a-glance overview of your project and the various sequences that you can amend and shuffle around as you progress, and possibly even provide as a rough sequence order for the edit.

Whilst the current template opens with the car crash, because it is a dramatic audience hook, a later version of the template – or even the completed film – might open with Dawn walking the streets telling us that she is terrified to leave her house, followed by a scene with her asleep in bed, followed by the dream as a delayed shock tactic, which vividly reveals just *why* she is terrified.

The template also gives you a chance to see where you might make good use of your story components and to consider any linking material that might be needed from your interviewees. If you are not planning to use a narration, for instance, some of the ideas and transitions may need setting up. A few additional questions to your contributors could well provide some useful material that will connect some of the ideas together so that there is more of a flow to the narrative.

It is advisable not to show this template to those who will be appearing in your film, or explain to them why you need certain information to help the film's flow. It is up to you to plan your questions carefully so that you can elicit a natural and honest response, without any answers being stage-managed or contrived. For the same reason, you should not show your interviewees a list of questions, even though you would have discussed with them the areas you plan to cover and their context within the film, and allow scenes such as the meeting and subsequent counselling sessions with Dr Myers to run naturally.

Amend the template as the content changes

In this particular example there will be little overall change between the initial template and completion of the film – but a dramatic turn of events will provide you with an unforeseen subtext and an unexpected resolution.

As the filming progresses you begin to wonder if Dawn's unfulfilled creative desires have led her to paint dramatic pictures in her own mind as a means of escape from the emotional torment. Then you make the discovery that her sister Claire was never involved in a car crash, though her parents were killed in a particularly dreadful one whilst holidaying abroad some years previously. It comes to light that Dawn has been unable to face the true horror of her parents' accident, feeling guilty about the rift, and subconsciously substituting her sister in the accident, thus causing an unsettled relationship between the two. Although Dawn agrees to a course of therapy, it seems likely the film will conclude that only reconciliation with Claire and an acceptance that her sister's accident really was only a dream, can ultimately begin the healing process.

Whilst this piece of exposition was not in the original template it is clearly a vital part of the story and a significant turning point. Inserting it in the film will be a matter of juxtaposition and restructuring, but you are not obliged to tell the story chronologically if you decide it is better to hold back information. You will not be distorting any of the interviewees' dialogue or the story itself – you will simply be preserving the subtext, thus making the revelation of Dawn's denial more dramatic. Light and shade, balance and texture, remember, are just as important to the telling of the story as the story itself.

DEVISING A SHOOTING SCRIPT FOR DRAMA SEQUENCES

Unlike the simple creative template you might use for a documentary, any scripted drama sequences will need translating into a detailed shooting script so that a filming schedule can be worked out.

It is irrelevant whether you are involved in a high-quality broadcast period piece or a low budget drama made with borrowed equipment and some willing actor friends. You will almost certainly not film every scene in one continuous shot and from only one angle, so you will need to devise an order of filming which takes on board any camera position changes, costume changes, set changes, lighting changes and continuity of action. Figure 7 (page 135) is from a typical drama scene.

This short scene, which features a youth worker and a teacher who is being threatened by a gang of young thugs, could be part of a complete drama, or a drama reconstruction flashback sequence in a documentary, as recalled by the teacher himself.

In the scene we establish that it is an interior, it is mid afternoon, that there are two characters, and some out-of-vision activity that is relevant to the scenario. This scene, however, will be sandwiched between several other scenes, possibly an earlier one when the youth worker first arrives, followed by a scene with the thugs discussing their plans. It might be followed by a later scene, at night, inside the same flat, when David returns having been seriously beaten up – to face an explosive encounter with his terrified wife.

SCENE 20: INT. DAY. INTERIOR DAVID'S FLAT. MID AFTERNOON

DAVID is staring out THE WINDOW at the street activity below. He turns away from the window to face TIM BARRETT, who is seated in an ARMCHAIR.

                              DAVID
                 I thought I might go and talk to them.

                              TIM
                 Talk to them? Are you mad?

                              DAVID
                           (defiantly)
                 Why not? They're only kids, what can I lose?

                              TIM
                 They carry knives and guns in their satchels, David,
                 and you don't want to know what damage they can
                 cause with an ordinary ballpoint pen.

DAVID considers this for a moment, then moves towards the door.

                              DAVID
                 I know there have been problems, but someone
                 needs to make contact with them. We're
                 responsible adults, Tim. If we can't help them,
                 who can?

                              TIM
                 Talk to them tomorrow when you've had a chance to
                 think things through.

                              DAVID
                 No. It'll be too late tomorrow. Far too late.

DAVID opens THE DOOR and exits, intent on resolving the situation.

Figure 7 Example of a drama script

Consider your filming options

In devising a shooting script you need to take on board various factors, bearing in mind that it is unlikely you will film the shots in the order they will be edited in. For a start, it may have taken two hours to light the master wide shot facing the window for the earlier scene that occurred seven or eight pages back when the youth worker first arrived at the flat. You would not want to move the camera and all your lights to film the reverses facing the armchair for that one scene, and then have to move everything back again and relight in order to film the later scene from an identical camera position.

The most time efficient method in these circumstances is to film a particular lighting set-up in one direction for *every* interior day scene inside the flat, and then reposition and relight for all the reverse shots for those scenes, matching the lighting and the continuity accordingly. It could be that the youth worker actor is only available for one day anyway, and you can't have him sitting around waiting for his reverses while you relight and shoot the master night scene, which he doesn't even feature in.

It might also be that the entire flat has been 'redecorated' in the story by some of the thugs, and the furniture smashed up, between the day scene and the night scene, in which case it would be easier to co-ordinate camera and design by shooting all the day scenes, changing the look of the entire set, then relighting for night.

It's much safer to shoot like this anyway, because if on viewing the rushes you decide you want to film some pick ups on the master day shot, you will not want to have ripped the entire set apart and changed the lighting between the two very different scenarios. It would also be a good idea to have at least two sets of identical clothing for David, one in good condition, the other torn and blood-stained, just in case of unforeseen retakes.

Devise a simple shooting script

Production companies will have their own individual layouts for a shooting script, depending on the complexity of the production. For a first film you should keep things as simple as possible, a basic shooting template for this story possibly looking something like Figure 8 on page 138.

Most drama productions will extract the actual scenes from the original script and re-order them so that the shooting script will have the complete dialogue running through the pages in the order in which they will be shot. It saves having to jump about all over the pages in the original script in order to find the scene you are currently working on.

Keep everyone in the loop

Whether they refer to the template or the shooting script itself, anyone involved in the production can see at a glance the order the scenes will be shot in, the actors who will be involved, what props are required, whether it's day or night, and any other requirements, such as specialist make-up.

Taking digital photos during the shoot will help you monitor continuity, and the beauty of digital recording is that you can always play back scenes to check both continuity of lighting and action, providing you have been noting down the timecodes for fast access for each of the scenes.

Being well organised gives everyone else a fighting chance to make their individual contributions to the production as part of a team, without confusion and without the need to be constantly asking you questions about what is going on.

SC	SET	D/N	ARTISTES	PROPS & NOTES
18	INT DAVID'S FLAT FACING WINDOW & DOOR	Day	Max Marshall Brian Hughes	Brian's briefcase
20	INT DAVID'S FLAT FACING WINDOW & DOOR	Day	Max Marshall Brian Hughes	Brian's briefcase
18	INT DAVID'S FLAT REVERSES	Day	Max Marshall Brian Hughes	Brian's briefcase
20	INT DAVID'S FLAT REVERSES	Day	Max Marshall Brian Hughes	Brian's briefcase
	BREAK FOR PAINTING OF SCENE FLATS			
22	INT DAVID'S FLAT FACING WINDOW & DOOR Set now covered in graffiti and furniture broken	Night	Max Marshall Patsy Sutton	Max make-up: Bruises, cuts and black eye. Clothing torn
22	INT DAVID'S FLAT REVERSES Set now covered in graffiti and furniture broken	Night	Max Marshall Patsy Sutton	Max make-up: Bruises, cuts and black eye. Clothing torn

Figure 8   Simple shooting script

11

Communication is Key

Good communication is fundamental to the success of your project. 'If only you'd told me that' are words you never want to hear during the course of your production. To avoid any misunderstandings you need to communicate with everyone.

THE COMMUNICATION HIT LIST

- Production manager
- Designer
- Cameraman
- Sound recordist
- First assistant director
- Electrician
- Artistes, actors, presenters
- Interviewees
- Expert contributors
- Location owners and proprietors
- Facilities houses.

Even if the production is a small one it is unlikely that the production team will consist entirely of you. Location proprietors and owners need to know the gameplan, as well as interviewees and anyone hiring equipment to you for the production, so it is unwise to under-estimate just how much organisation will be needed.

Arrange a production meeting

Whether it's you and a few mates meeting in a bedroom, or a full-blown gathering of production personnel at a broadcast company, a production meeting is the best opportunity you will have to talk through every aspect of the project to those who will be involved. Key personnel should attend the meeting – usually a production manager, cameraman, sound recordist and designer – and this should be arranged soon after the recce has taken place, assuming that most of the story elements have been identified by then.

Ahead of the meeting you should:

- draft your budget
- complete an outline shooting schedule
- photocopy any treatments, scripts or storyboards for distribution
- collate and photocopy any relevant information ready for distribution
- organise your audition/recce photographs for discussion.

Your budget and shooting schedule do not need to be fixed in stone at this stage, since discussion at the meeting could well throw up some items that need to be factored in, but you should have a reasonably good idea of what it will cost and how long it will take.

BUDGET YOUR FILM SENSIBLY

Even if your film is a low-budget production, your expenditure can still escalate if you do not agree your costs in advance and list them for reference and amendment. If you are using your own equipment, including editing software, have no travel costs, and your interviewees and locations are free, then it's possible your budget will achieve enviable status. But once you start factoring in any costs over and above the freebies, you will need to keep a close eye on your cash flow.

If you are making your film with any kind of financial backing, the backer, or broadcaster, will expect you to provide a realistic and accurate budget as a condition of the agreement. In such circumstances, the budget should be broken down into sections, such as Script Development, Artistes, Production Unit, Unit Crew, Editing, and so on, with each section's sub-total automatically updating the grand total. In this way you can control your costs, adding an extra shoot day, perhaps, whilst reducing a couple of edit days, with an at-a-glance review of the effect and implications of this on both the individual items and the overall budgeted cost.

A typical section of a basic budget, formulated in Excel, might look something like Figure 9 (pages 142–3).

Creating your own budget template using available spreadsheet software is perfectly acceptable if you are making your own low-budget film, though specially designed packages such as Movie Magic Budgeting, Movietools, Easy Budget, or CompanyMOVE budgeting are available for more advanced users. For a first film you should not need to splash out on budgeting software just yet but, whatever system you use, itemise *everything* that has a cost implication and constantly review your options.

DEVISE A REALISTIC SHOOTING SCHEDULE

With the recce completed, agreements in place and budget and shooting script now available, you need to draw up your shooting

SCHEDULE 5

STORY/SCRIPT/DEVELOPMENT	RATE	PRE WEEKS	PROD'N DAYS	POST DAYS	CLEAR WEEKS	TOTAL £
DEVELOPMENT	500					500
RIGHTS/OPTIONS/PAYMENTS						
SCRIPTWRITER/LINKS						
Total:						500

SCHEDULE 6

PRODUCER/DIRECTORS (WEEKLY)	RATE	PRE WEEKS	PROD'N DAYS	POST DAYS	CLEAR WEEKS	TOTAL £
EXECUTIVE PRODUCER						
PRODUCER/DIRECTOR (WEEKLY)	875	5	12	26		7000
RESEARCHER/AP (DAILY)	150		4			600
RESEARCH & LOCATIONS						
Total:						8000

Figure 9   Budget spreadsheet

SCHEDULE 7

ARTISTES	RATE	RHL WEEKS	PROD'N DAYS	DUBBING DAYS	CLEAR DAYS	TOTAL £
MAIN ARTISTES						
WALK-ON 1						
WALK-ON 2						
Total:						0

SCHEDULE 8

PRESENTERS/INTERVIEWEES	RATE	RHL DAYS	PROD'N DAYS	DUBBING DAYS	CLEAR DAYS	TOTAL £
PRESENTER (DAILY)	500		10			5000
GUESTS/EXPERTS						2200
PARTICIPANTS						1000
Total:						8200

SCHEDULE 9

PRODUCTION UNIT SALARIES	RATE	PRE WEEKS	PROD'N DAYS	POST DAYS	CLEAR DAYS	TOTAL £
PROD MANAGER (WEEKLY)	800	8				6400
PROD SECRETARY (WEEKLY)	200	4				
PROD RUNNER (WEEKLY)						800
Total:						7200

Figure 9   Budget spreadsheet (continued)

schedule. Over and above everything else the schedule needs to be realistic. Everything on a shoot takes longer than you think – even for seasoned professionals – so you should leave nothing to chance, always allowing plenty of time for:

- travel to the first location
- travel between locations
- set-up and wrap at each location
- rehearsals with presenters and actors
- make-up and wardrobe
- pre-filming chat with interviewees
- props and set dressing
- weather and environmental changes
- other factors, such as animals and children.

You also need to analyse the most efficient way to approach each filming day, taking on board time between locations or set-ups against availability of performers, interviewees, props and any activity out of your control that may need working around: a theme park that will not let you access certain rides until the gates are closed to the public, for example, or a factory where you need to film the start of a process and the end result, sandwiching an interview with the Managing Director in between, before he flies off for that crucial meeting in Hamburg.

And remember the earlier example we looked at of a crew filming a chase sequence on a mountainside. It really does make sense to schedule multiple scenes within one location whenever you can so that you don't need to move people and equipment about unnecessarily.

Make your schedule cost-effective

You don't need to be halfway up a mountain to be time efficient of course. If you use your time wisely on the recce, you will know by the time you come to schedule that you can film an interview inside a restaurant in the morning, then a park scene just around the corner before lunch, and an office scene just two blocks away in the afternoon. This means the electricians can be moving the lights from the restaurant to the office and setting them up whilst you are away filming in the park.

Make sure that you schedule any establishers or incidental cutaways after the main shoot if at all possible, and remember to build in breaks for tea, coffee and lunch. You cannot push people to extremes, or you will risk trying their patience and losing their goodwill, both often a saving grace when unforeseen problems descend on you and everyone needs to pull together to get the film back on track.

You will also need to decide if taking on a runner or a First Assistant Director (First AD) would be cost-effective, and if some pressure could be taken off the main shoot by having a second camera to pick up crucial cutaways and complementary scenes. Our previous scenario of the rock band on the road would positively benefit from having a two camera unit, not only for giving better overall coverage of the rehearsals and stage performances, but being on standby to follow any sudden behind-the-scenes-activity that may otherwise have been missed.

Apply logic and co-ordination to your schedule

For our *Dream World* scenario we would clearly want to schedule the Dawn and Claire interviews close together as they live in the same town, though that may not mean they would both be around at the same time, in which case a convenient date would need to be co-ordinated. The meeting with Dr Myers would need to be arranged when both he and Dawn are available, though the trip to Scotland itself could be filmed after the event if necessary, and the surreal dream scenarios, including the car crash, could be scheduled for almost any time.

You will need, however, to weigh up how Dawn might be affected by the meeting with Dr Myers. Filming the sequences chronologically means that you will have Dawn feeling fresh and positive at least up to that meeting. But if you schedule any scenes with her *after* the Dr Myers meeting and a solution for her problem is not forthcoming, she may become depressed and pessimistic about the future and her enthusiasm and co-operation may dissolve, along with your unfinished scenes.

Scheduling, therefore, has to take into account any number of permutations and any number of factors, including practical, financial, and sometimes emotive. The schedule documents themselves have varying degrees of complexity, particularly when drama is involved. A basic schedule for *Dream World* might look like Figure 10 (page 147).

The realities of scheduling

At some stage this basic schedule will need to be converted into a detailed Call Sheet, showing meeting times, location addresses, hotel addresses for overnight stays, contact telephone numbers and so on, but for now it serves as an overview of the order you plan to film the various scenes in and the dates on which they will be shot.

DATE	LOCATION	SCENES	CONTRIBUTORS
May 2	London	Sufferer interview	Matthew Price
	London	Sufferer interview	Arlene May
May 3	Birmingham	Sufferer interview	Brian Shelgrave
	Nottingham	Sufferer interview	Sarah Channing
May 4	Manchester	Main interview 1	Dawn
	Manchester	Dawn asleep in bed Dawn out shopping Dawn's photographs Dawn's home movies	Dawn
	Manchester	Main interview 2 Claire's photographs	Claire
May 5	Manchester to Stirling	The car journey to Scotland	Dawn
May 6	Arrival in Stirling	Sufferer interview	Julie Seaton
	Stirling	Location establishers Main interview 3 Dr Myers at work The first meeting	Dr Sean Myers Dawn
May 8	Stirling	Consultation 1	Dawn and Sean Myers
May 9	Stirling	Consultation 2	Dawn and Sean Myers
May 10	Stirling to Manchester	Dream recreations: Cornfield Seashore Loch Building site	
May 12	Manchester to London	Dream recreation Pick-ups if needed	

Figure 10 *Dream World* **shooting schedule**

You might have elected to start with the car crash recreation and some of the dream recreations to get your creative juices flowing, but do you have enough information to do the sequences justice? Although you have spoken briefly to each of the sufferers and possibly have an image of their dreams in your head, until you interview them you will not have a particularly vivid account, and some of the scenarios may well change in the telling. In any event, this is a deep and difficult subject and before talking to Dawn and Dr Myers, it would be a good idea to become as informed as possible about the complexities of the problem and the ramifications for those who suffer.

Assess the geographical implications of your shoot

As a general rule, it is always wise to conduct your interviews first anyway so that you can make notes of relevant cutaways and complementary scenes you might need to film, otherwise there is a strong possibility you will find yourself going back to a location to film pick-ups. You schedule the interviews, taking into account the respective geographical progression between each location point, in this case starting in London, moving on to Birmingham, then Nottingham, and finally Manchester, where you will meet up separately with Dawn and Claire.

You have allowed two days for the next phase of the schedule, which involves filming Dawn's car journey to Scotland, including various stop-offs in order to film a combination of some preconceived and off-the-top-of-your-head 'fantasy' dream scenarios. Depending on how many people are involved in the filming – all of whom will need to spend several nights in a hotel or B & B – you may elect to remove one day from the schedule and attempt the car journey in one day so that you can cut down on costs.

Upon arrival in Stirling you will film another sufferer that Dr Myers has recommended and then interview Myers himself the following day, but without Dawn being present because you want their first meeting to be natural and spontaneous. Having filmed cutaways of Dr Myers at work, you bring Dawn back and record their initial meeting and discussion, then film the various consultations over the next two days as observational sequences.

You will work your way back down from Stirling to Manchester, then London, stopping en route to film the dream recreations at appropriate locations you may have come across, and noted, on the way up. These are obviously not detailed scenarios. Hand-held shots will suffice; abstract images of walking through cornfields and wading through water can be treated in post-production to give an eerie fantasy look that will texture your story and offer visual relief from a succession of on-camera interviews. And then you cross your fingers that everything goes according to plan.

PROTECT YOURSELF AGAINST THE UNEXPECTED

Before you start distributing documentation and organising a meeting, there is one other important item you will need to address: do you need insurance and, if so, how much do you need?

Well, the short answer is yes, you really should have insurance, particularly if you are out and about filming among the public, or on private property, or with actors. The location days might go like a dream, and without any mishaps, but are you willing to take the chance?

Even if you are working by yourself or with a group of friends, accidents can happen and you may regret not having any cover. If you are making a film for a production company, a studio, or a broadcaster, they will require you to have appropriate insurance cover, and would be able to help with the arrangements.

There are various types of insurance cover, not all of which may apply to you:

■ public liability insurance
■ equipment cover
■ negative and videotape insurance
■ props, sets and wardrobe insurance
■ employers liability insurance.

Deciding which insurance cover you may need

Public liability insurance is one thing you need to have, and is a legal requirement. If somebody trips over a trailing cable, or a lighting stand falls and knocks them unconscious, the law will hold you responsible. If members of the public, including people you are interviewing, file a valid claim and you are not insured, it could prove costly. Public liability insurance provides your production with cover in case of bodily injury or property damage to them during the course of the production.

Hired equipment insurance covers you for loss or damage to any equipment you may be hiring from a facilities company. The company will require proof that the equipment is covered before hiring it out, and in most instances, you should be able to arrange insurance through them, or with an insurer they recommend.

Negative and videotape insurance protects you against loss or damage to your film or videotape stock during production and post-production. It could also cover you against re-filming scenes which have been lost as a result of faulty stock, a faulty camera, or faulty processing.

Props, sets and wardrobe insurance will be needed if you are hiring props or wardrobe and will also cover you if you own any of the items yourself. If you are filming in a museum or a historic building you may be required to have insurance that reflects replacement costs for loss or damage.

Employers liability insurance is a legal requirement if you are employing, or paying, any members of your unit. It insures them in the event of bodily injury, disease, death or illness whilst working on your film.

Proof of insurance will be required by local authorities, studios and location owners, as well as facilities houses, so it is advisable to carry the documents with you at all times.

Making contact with an insurance company

You should contact an insurance broker – preferably one who deals with entertainment-related insurance – well in advance of filming, giving them as much information as possible about the shoot, the people involved, and the locations. There are far too many potential problems waiting to disrupt your project without you having to worry about unexpected accidents, so it makes sense to pay for some peace of mind.

Contact details of specialist insurance companies can be found in numerous trade directories, including *The Knowledge*, *Kemps* and *Kays Production Manual*.

MAKING THE MOST OF A PRODUCTION MEETING

So now you're almost ready to go out filming. On your own if it's a one-person shoot, but if not, it's time to share out your accumulated knowledge by inviting your friends and helpers round for an update in your living room, or arranging a formal meeting with key members of the production team around an office table.

A typical agenda might be:

■ present a general overview of the proposed film
■ hand out a shooting schedule for discussion
■ show your audition/recce photographs
■ hand out floor plans if you have any
■ outline what you have discovered at the recce
■ discuss the general visual treatment of the film
■ discuss your equipment requirements
■ discuss any design requirements
■ discuss any possible additional requirements
■ distribute call sheets
■ hand out a treatment and proposal if you have one
■ hand out scripts if you have them.

Begin with an overview

It is always best to start by giving an overview of the project; the story, the central character, or characters, and the approach you intend to take, be it humorous, investigative, abstract, stylised or emotionally charged. Then describe the components that will shape the story, be they interviews, action sequences, observational sequences, fantasy sequences, dramatic recreations, or archive footage.

Giving a broad brushstroke of the film helps you to avoid giving away too much detail too soon and risking overwhelming everyone. Start small and build the idea, along with your enthusiasm, so that the rest of the team can see the story unfold before they turn their attention to the detail. Then ask if there are any general questions. Everyone's input should be given due consideration, because there may be things you have missed, or you may have got too close to your subject matter at this point and an injection of fresh thinking could prove useful.

Expand the idea into specifics

If you have written up a treatment or a proposal, or have a script, you should hand these out at the end of the session so that everyone can stay focused during the meeting. Give as much detail as possible about the kind of characters in the film and how you think they will shape the story. Hand out any photos of contributors or actors so that the team can become more familiar with the people who will be driving the film's narrative.

You should then describe any visual treatment the film might require. You may have decided to give it a raw, grainy look, or a soft dream-like quality, or a combination of filming styles and techniques. If someone other than you has responsibility for camerawork and lighting they need to be able to share your vision as early as possible as it may have implications on your equipment list – lenses and filters, for instance – and post-production work. In most instances, visual treatment is best left until the editing stage, when you can choose a distinctive look from literally hundreds that are available. As the possibilities are discussed at the meeting you may decide you will need an extra edit day to achieve the look you want, and that may have cost implications.

The shooting schedule as a catalyst for discussion

Next, distribute a shooting schedule so that the assembled group can see how long the filming is going to take, how many locations there are, how much movement there will be between locations, and the number of scenes you are hoping to film each day. This will doubtless provoke lively debate as everyone assesses the implications and puts forward concerns and suggestions. This is when you may find yourself tweaking or adapting the schedule, and various cost implications may need to be taken on board.

Many of these questions might be answered by looking over your recce photographs and rough 'floor plans'. You may already have considered some of these problems and can put forward solutions for some, and request ideas and suggestions for others.

What kind of tracking equipment would be most suitable for a particular terrain? Would two cameras give better coverage? Do you need a First AD or a runner to help organise any crowds or onlookers? Would walkie talkies be useful? Can back-up equipment be arranged in case of technical breakdowns? Will the sound recordist be okay with just a gun mike or will radio mikes be needed? And distributing a props and wardrobe list could be very useful, as each member of the team can suggest any items that they can contribute to avoid having to hire them or purchase them especially for the shoot.

Remember, the purpose of the meeting is to share knowledge, assess potential problems and devise the best solutions. Having established strong lines of communication you need to ensure that they remain tight throughout the pre-production phase, during the shoot, and right up to post-production.

CALL SHEETS MAINTAIN STRONG COMMUNICATION

All production companies create and distribute a call sheet just prior to filming and there is no reason for you to think that you won't need one just because yours is a low-budget film devoid of any complex scenes, or armies of actors and extras, and with everything under complete control.

You would be amazed at how many incidents I can think of where members of a film unit have gone out on shoots having left behind a vital piece of equipment, with no contact number to call so they can retrieve it, or have lost contact with a member of the unit because their mobile number had changed without anyone being told, or they were found wandering around looking for a location because they had neither a map nor a contact number with which to get directions.

Successful shoots are invariably those that are well organised and where nothing is left to chance. Let's look at a typical call sheet (Figure 11, pages 156–7) for a day's filming on *Smoke and Mirrors*, a drama documentary involving interviews, performance, establishers, archive footage and drama reconstructions.

Anyone receiving this Call Sheet from the producer or the production office will be left in no doubt as to where the locations are, what time they are supposed to be at those locations, and who to ring in case contact needs to be made with anyone, urgently or otherwise. All information relating to lunch, first aid, emergency contacts, health and safety, parking facilities, and on-camera interviewees is also listed.

The Call Sheet is for a documentary segment, involving interviews with a magic historian and The Great Bodini's biographer, and a

ANYTIME PRODUCTIONS CALL SHEET

Title: Smoke and Mirrors
Producer: Lucy Golden
Production Office: 01234 567

Production Mobiles:
Director: Hans Tyler (01234 568)
Cameraman: Dick Stone (01234 569)
Sound engineer: Martin Rickman (01234 570)
Electrician: Roy Tebbitt (01234 571)
Historian: Ellie Simpson
Biographer: Ben Chamberlain
Cat & Whistle: See map for details

Calltimes: Unit call: 08.30 at location, Tuesday 5 June 200X
                              Lunch: 13.00, then wrap and travel to Bell's Marina,
                              Norwich
Weather: Temp: 16 degrees, light rain pm
                              Sunrise; 05.45 Sunset: 21.30

Locations:
Rectory, Dingley Thorpe, Norfolk (see map). Contact: Sarah Brown 01603 444 XXX
Bells Marina, Waterside, Norwich (see map). Contact: Stephen Grey 01603 222 XXX

Scene	Set and synopsis	Day/Night	Contributors
1	Interior rectory, The Great Bodini's birthplace	day	
2	Interview with magic historian	day	Ellie Simpson
3	Establishers Dingley Thorpe and VOX POPS	day	Local inhabitants
4	Establishers marina and site of Bodini's great crate escape	day	
5	Interview with Bodini's biographer	day	Ben Chamberlain

Figure 11   Call sheet (1)

Camera	Flynn Equipment Hire Contact: Ryder Houseman on 07889 224 667
Sound	Sounds Fantastic Contact: Slim Benton on 08781 999 444
Emergency Contacts	Local hospital: Norwich and Norfolk Local police: Norwich
First Aider	Sarah Bellman will be present all day
Fluorescent jackets	Available from the crew van. Must be worn whilst filming all street scenes.
Safety and Risk Assessments	Copies of Risk Assessment available through the director. Please read before filming commences.

Please note:

No food or drink to be consumed on set.

No smoking allowed on set.

Alcohol consumption will not be permitted at any time.

Please bring only essential vehicles as there is limited parking.

Director's notes:

There are no catering facilities at Dingley Thorpe. Lunch at the Cat & Whistle.

There is limited natural light inside the church but ample power points.

Whilst filming at Bell's Marina we must observe the company's health and safety guidelines.

Life jackets and hard hats must be worn at the Marina.

Figure 11   Call sheet (1) (continued)

scene looking at the site of one of his great water escape tricks.

The example (Figure 12, pages 159–60) is a filming day concentrating on two drama segments.

Whenever artists are involved, everything takes that much longer. As you can see from the call sheet, although the camera crew are due on site at 0800 to set and light, two of the performers are being collected at 0600 so that costume and make-up can be attended to before they face the cameras. Then there will be rehearsal time for the actors and the design department, who will need to check that all the props are working properly.

Whether you are planning a complex shoot or something much more straightforward, discussing your plans at a production meeting then imparting detailed information by means of a call sheet will keep communications tight so that no one will ever have any reason to say 'If only you'd told me that'.

ANYTIME PRODUCTIONS CALL SHEET

Title: Smoke and Mirrors
Producer: Lucy Golden
Production Office: 01206 777 XXX

Production Mobiles:
Director: Hans Tyler (01234 568)
Cameraman: Dick Stone (01234 569)
Sound engineer: Martin Rickman (01234 570)
Electrician: Roy Tebbitt (01234 571)
Designer: Gwen Sellars (01234 572)
Make-up: Linda Grant (01234 573)
Wardrobe: John Friedland (01234 574)
Magic adviser: Edwardo The Magnificent
Bon Appetite Caterers

Calltimes: Unit call: 08.00 at location, Thursday 14 June 200X
                    Lunch: 12.30 Wrap at 19.00
Weather: Temp: 18 degrees, cloudy
                    Sunrise: 05.45 Sunset: 21.30

Location:
The Magic Emporium 333 444 XXX

Scene	Set and synopsis	Script pages	D/N	Characters
4	Exterior theatre. Bodini argues with his manager	12/13	day	The Great Bodini Arthur Bennett
6	Interior theatre. Bodini performs the Exploding Head trick	16/17	night	The Great Bodini Bodini's assistant

Figure 12   Call sheet (2)

Artist	Character	Pick Up	Costume	Make-up	On Set
John Rickman	Bodini	0600	0700	0800	0100
David Argent	Manager	0630	0700	0900	0100
Julie Lightfoot	Assistant	1000	1100	1200	1400

Camera	Flynn Equipment Hire Contact: Ryder Houseman on 01234 575
Sound	Sounds Fantastic Contact: Slim Benton on 01234 576
Magic Props	The Magic House, Coventry Contact: Stan Delaware
Emergency Contacts	Local hospital: Deniston, A&E Local police: Deniston Road
Additional equipment	Hollywood track for both scenes
Safety and Risk Assessments	Copies of Risk Assessment available through the director. Please read them before filming commences.

Please note:

No food or drink to be consumed on set.

No smoking allowed on set.

Alcohol consumption will not be permitted at any time.

Director's notes:
Only performers and magic adviser are permitted to handle the magic props.

Figure 12 Call sheet (2) (continued)

12

Practical Magic

The debate that raged on for years was 'do we use film or video?'
This, of course, was before the digital revolution brought with it
even greater choice and forced us to look at video and film-making
in a number of different ways.

FILM OR NEW MEDIA

Whilst film still has a unique role to play in cinema and in
broadcast, it is videotape that is facing the biggest challenges from
new media applications. DVDs, hard drives and memory cards
with amazing capacity have all mounted a technological assault
on one of our most revered forms of communication, reducing
large spools of moving tape to a static, virtually unseen, vehicle of
information, education and entertainment. This is good news for
anyone wishing to express themselves in the world of audio visual
interaction, because the means to transmit ideas, thoughts and
feelings throughout the human network have become cheaper,
faster and much more accessible.

Film stands its ground

There are many, of course, who would wish to use no other form
of mass communication than the beloved medium of film. It was
where it all began, after all, and remains to this day rich in visual

depth and texture, with a quality that has only been challenged in recent years by the advent of High Definition.

Why else would millions of drama and documentary-makers take their videotape rushes to edit suites worldwide and ask the editor to 'give them a film look'? And many of us still refer to the process of capturing and editing moving images, in whatever format, as 'making a film', in homage to the origins of this endlessly fascinating craft.

Unlike videotape or memory cards, you can still hold film up to the light and marvel at the ingenuity behind those little photographic images imprinted onto celluloid, then physically edit the pictures together and run them through a projector to bring them flickering magically to life. But today, using film comes at a price.

Film as an option

Whilst film does still remain a viable option, it is a comparatively expensive one. As demand falls, material costs rise; compare the price of a one-hour Mini DV tape to the equivalent in film stock. Add to that the processing costs of producing a negative and then a positive print with which to work, and your budget can start to wobble at the knees – especially if you've gone on location and wildly overshot everything.

When you run film through the camera you cannot see precisely what you are getting, although video assist has given the cameraman and director the means to playback scenes in recent years. And whether you are using 8mm, 16mm, Super 16mm or 35mm, film does not record sound directly on to the celluloid, but to a separate DAT tape, linked by a cable between the camera and the sound recording equipment, and synchronised by a signal from the camera to keep them both frame accurate. This means you will need to synch your 'rushes' after filming by lining up the sound – transferred to magnetic film stock with identical sprocket holes – with the picture, with the aid of an in vision hand clap or a clapper board.

Many film directors and producers are not deterred by such minor inconveniences, preferring to humour the new kids on the block and stick with the tried and tested excellence of the creative medium they hold in the highest regard, complete with all its historical connections and romantic connotations. Though they can, of course, shoot on film and post produce entirely digitally, which is an option preferred by many who elect to exploit both mediums to best advantage.

The growing popularity of new media

Romantic and creative preferences aside, however, there are huge practical advantages in using the new media technologies. When videotape first barged its way onto the scene there were discernible differences of opinion between the creatives and the engineers as to who had control of the new communications tool. Fortunately, everyone soon recognised the contribution that each could make, and the ensuing growth of audio visual equipment and software has created a veritable magic playground, filled with a range of exciting toys that offer us extraordinary flexibility and choice.

CHOOSING THE RIGHT CAMERA

Although buying or hiring a camera that suits both your pocket and your creative aspirations is important, the true quality of the film you make will be evident in the way you structure and tell your story, its imagery enhanced by the resolution and picture quality of the camera in conjunction with the lighting. Your film could be a widescreen spectacular filmed to visual perfection and splendour, but if it is not compelling for the audience, its purpose as a conveyor of entertainment will be immediately devalued.

Many successful features in recent years have been filmed using video cameras, for example *28 Days Later,* filmed on a Canon XL1. And remember the short film *Dog Years,* filmed with an 8mm camera on grainy film stock and edited in camera to produce a highly entertaining and engaging story. Further back, there is Ken Russell's strikingly inventive *Amelia and the Angel,* funded by the BFI Experimental Fund and shot with a borrowed, mute, 16mm camera using black and white stock, with a soundtrack added in the edit.

The camera cannot disguise any lack of inspiration or creative aptitude that a film-maker possesses in order to tell a story well, but by getting to know just what your camera is capable of, you can at least dispense your creative vision with images that hold focus whilst displaying an acceptable level of technical competence. Then you can move on to develop your skills so that ultimately your films will combine high levels of both creative and technical ability.

If film is your choice of format, the hire and purchase costs can be high – the cameras most favoured by professional cameramen being the Arriflex, Aaton or Eclair, with the Bolex being a reliable and trusted friend to professional and amateur alike. It has to be said, however, that film these days is regarded as something of a specialist medium, using specialist lenses and specialist skills, and probably not the first option that any emerging director would go for in the digital world of choice and low-budget production.

Giving yourself flexible options

The reason why digital technology has become so popular in recent years is obvious: a wide range of affordable, accessible cameras; cheap stock (even more cost effective when recording directly onto erasable memory cards or a hard drive); ease of use; instant playback for reviewing rushes, and immediate integration with computer editing systems.

Firstly, you need to decide what type of camera you can afford, especially if your first film is more of a learning curve than a full-bodied creative offensive. The choice of digital camcorders available on the high street is enormous and you can always check out the camera's specifications on the web or any of the camcorder review magazines before parting with any hard cash. All the top manufacturers, including Sony, Panasonic and Canon make cameras at entry level, as well as for semi-professional and professional use.

Even though today's camcorder technology moves extraordinarily fast and the currently available options will be replaced with new products within a few months, there will always be certain specifications that, as a film-maker, you will need to consider, dependent on your individual needs.

You do *not* need a camera that can do flashy special effects, or subtitle in multiple languages, or offers in-camera editing facilities. It should certainly be DV format and not analogue and, whatever format it records to, be sure that the camera will either output the content directly onto your computer for editing via the industry standard FireWire connectivity, or to a video capture card. If not, make sure that its recorded content can at least output to a computer via a secondary device such as an external hard drive (for example the Fire Store products, which can record up to 7 hours of DV material) or a DVD player.

The best starting point, then, is deciding on the format:

- DVD
- Memory card
- Hard drive
- Mini DV.

CHOOSING THE FORMAT THAT'S RIGHT FOR YOU

DVD is a format familiar to most of us but the DVDs used in camcorders, though inexpensive, have a much more limited record time, 20 minutes or so at acceptable quality, which means they have to be switched for blank discs at relatively short intervals. Possibly not the most popular format choice in the long run for normal digital camcorders, though dual layer High Definition DVD recording cameras are about to effect a change, with Sony investing heavily in XDCAM tech, which is essentially the same Blu-ray DVD you can play in a PS3.

Memory cards can be expensive to buy, particularly those with the highest storage capacity – and you would need the highest available. Unfortunately, a high quality setting takes up an enormous amount of memory space. In order to increase the storage capacity you would need high compression, which would produce a lower quality image. Memory cards are, however, in a relatively early stage of development and their performance and storage capacity is almost certain to improve in the coming years.

Many of us have experienced the benefits of large hard drive capacity on our computers and television recorders, and those built into camcorders can be between 80GB and 100GB, which is enough storage for over 20 hours of recording at the highest quality level. If you intend to shoot more than that, or hang on to your recorded material for any length of time, you'll need a camera with a detachable hard drive, or be able to download the material to a secondary format, such as DVD, an external hard drive, or as a digital file on your computer. If you choose a camcorder with a smaller hard drive you do not want to be archiving from your camcorder on location, so maximising your storage capability is certainly an important consideration.

The Mini DV is currently a hugely popular choice, using small cassette tapes that store up to 50 minutes of record time and used for both standard and HDV formats. For video editing, Mini DV produces better video image quality than many other formats (500 lines of resolution and CD quality stereo sound) and is available to buy through a wide variety of retail outlets. The tapes, however, unlike memory cards, hard drives and rewritable DVDs, should be used only once for maximum performance. You should also transfer the content as soon as possible to your computer, as viewing it directly on a camcorder causes unnecessary wear and tear on both the tapes and the machine.

FINDING YOUR WAY THROUGH THE DIGITAL MAZE

With so much choice it's easy to be confused, so the best advice is to go for the best that you can afford, knowing that if your initial ventures are successful, you can always trade up later to a camera that will give you more options and better picture quality.

The consumer camcorder route

If you decide to start by investing in a consumer digital

camcorder, check that it has audio video output so that you can transfer your rushes to your PC or Mac (or to an external hard drive servicing your computer), is PAL format, has image stabilisation in order to eliminate shakiness when filming hand-held scenes, and a zoom lens for capturing shots when you cannot get close enough to the action. Be wary, though, a zoom lens used as an actual zoom in a film can relegate your efforts very quickly to the status of a home movie. Use sparingly, covering your material on a tripod, a track, or as a hand-held shot.

With a basic camcorder you may find that you do not have an output for a directional microphone, having to rely solely on the fixed camera mic to record sound, and most consumer camcorders come with Autofocus, which means you literally point and shoot. There are serious drawbacks, however, in that your shots will drift in and out of focus as the lens settles on a selected subject, and you will have no control over exposure or where you want the exact point of focus to be.

The intermediate route

If you want more flexibility you will need to step up to intermediate, or semi-pro, level, and although these cameras are more expensive, you always have the option to hire them. More manual features means you will have much greater control over everything that you film, some of the settings being selected, modified and saved via an on-screen menu.

Typical features might include:

- white balance
- manual focus
- manual iris

- lens adapters
- filter ring
- external microphone input
- headphone jack
- audio metering
- time code
- FireWire/iLink DV in-and-out connection
- ability to switch between manual and auto settings.

Maintaining maximum control during filming

A white balance facility helps you control the colour balance of your shots. Different types of light have different colour wavelengths, daylight being towards the blue end of the spectrum, indoor lighting giving off a very yellow, or warm, light. In all lighting conditions you will have much more control over the colours being recorded, particularly in mixed lighting conditions, where you may have sunlight and practical lighting within the same shot. But you'll need to remember to check your white balance with every scene change or any change in lighting conditions.

Combining your technical resources with creative thinking

Manual focus gives you the option to choose your desired point of focus within the frame, allowing you to achieve more complex and creative shots. Shallow depth of field, for instance, in which the foreground remains sharp whilst the background stays soft (or vice versa), is achieved using a long lens (telephoto), whilst a shorter lens (wide angle) gives you more depth of field, whereby almost everything is in focus.

Using a long lens means you need to be particularly careful, because your focus becomes much more critical. However, it can be very useful in an interview situation, for example, when you want your interviewee to be sharp, and the background thrown into soft focus to make the shot composition more interesting, or possibly masking any unwanted background distractions.

Whilst only professional cameras can facilitate removable lenses, you can use lens adapters on many intermediate cameras, which give you the option to record both telephoto and wide angle shots.

Having the ability to manually adjust the iris allows you to expose your shots correctly, whereas auto exposure would not allow you as much control over the shot, under-exposing a foreground, for instance, if the background is too bright, thereby making a subject's face too dark. Opening the iris lets in more light, thus increasing the brightness; closing the iris makes the image darker. Some cameras have a facility to find out if you are over-exposing. This is a zebra pattern, which is overlaid over any white areas in the scene to help you adjust the exposure.

Manual control over shutter speeds is also useful. A fast shutter setting will make images sharp even if the subject is moving, whilst with a slow shutter setting the camera will take in more light, which is ideal for filming in low-light conditions.

A filter holder, matte box, or filter wheel would give you the added advantage of adding filters in front of, or behind, the lens, such as an AV filter to protect it from scratches, or specialised star filters to create starbursts, glows and various effects to enhance the creative look of your film – but you should use these with care. Shooting 'clean' footage at least gives you the option to add visual effects at the editing stage, without committing yourself on the shoot. A polarising filter, however, can reduce or eliminate reflections in water, windows and glass, since natural light bounces around all over the place, mostly out of your control.

Your camcorder would also benefit from having an input for an external microphone, audio metering, and a headphone jack to monitor the sound as it is being recorded to maintain good sound recording levels and to avoid distort. The camera should also have time code, and a FireWire/iLink DV in-and-out connection.

Whilst it is always better to have maximum control over your filming, it is nevertheless advisable to film with a camera that has the ability to use both manual settings and auto, since some situations might give you little or no time for setting up, and certain scenes may need to be recorded with 'on the hoof' immediacy and without any delay.

STAYING FUTURE PROOF

As the technology that allows us to record and edit moving pictures moves forward at a staggering rate, we need to be aware of what options are available and endeavour to embrace them whenever we can. Filming in standard 4:3 format, for example, is more or less confined to history, the widescreen format 16:9 now accepted as the norm. Not only are most cameras and editing software used exclusively for 16:9, audiences worldwide expect to watch a widescreen presentation and can be disappointed with anything less.

High Definition is the latest innovation designed to enhance our viewing experience, offering sound and pictures of outstanding quality. There is no immediate panic for a first time film-maker to rush out and invest in HDV equipment, since 16:9 formats produced on current camcorders will be around for many years to come. HDV cameras can even use the same standard Mini DV tapes, though offering much higher resolution. It is worth reflecting, however, that such impressive picture quality demands greater attention to lighting as it can show up visual blemishes in finer detail and whilst perfection is an ultimate goal, gaining experience in handling the basic features of camera and sound is still a very worthy investment.

As the years progress, High Definition will almost certainly become the chosen choice, the equipment becoming more accessible and less expensive and ultimately well worth stepping up to. At the end of the day, however, it is the quality of your story and the way you execute it which is paramount, and that should be your number one priority over and above everything else.

BEING PREPARED FOR A SHOOT

Leaving your base and setting off on a shoot without the proper equipment is not only extremely silly, it will inevitably cause delays, set you behind schedule and cause unnecessary frustration. You should always undertake an equipment check before you box-and-bag it, ticking off the items if necessary to be doubly sure that everything you need is there.

Typical equipment for a digital shoot might comprise:

- digital camera
- charger and power supply for camera
- 2 batteries, fully charged

- tripod (with a fluid head if possible)
- set of lights
- coloured filters (gels) to cover lights or windows to alter colour balance
- reflectors or white polystyrene
- Sennheiser directional mic and cable
- boom pole for the mic and cable
- portable sound mixer to control the sound balance
- headphones
- rain covers
- set of radio mics
- blank Mini DV cassettes (or other recordable media)
- additional monitor to check picture quality or visual framing.

LIGHTING TECHNIQUES

As discussed earlier, fast moving documentary shoots do not always have time for meticulous lighting, but there will be occasions when setting up lights is necessary, and if you are filming interior drama sequences you will almost certainly have to light them. The mood, the ambience and the tone of each scene you film, in fact, can be changed or enhanced in the way you use lights, sometimes in combination with props and set design.

Unless it is a stylised scene employing a particular lighting technique, the secret is to establish a mood, whilst creating an illusion of reality, without imposing itself on the viewer. Action should blend effortlessly within a scenario, so that we are not aware that the lighting has been manipulated to conjure up such an illusion – particularly in factual films where harsh reality may have to take centre stage and any suggestion of 'artistic' lighting would be entirely inappropriate. With drama you should be careful not to over-light because such scenes also need to appear as naturalistic as possible.

In any situation, whether using natural light or generated light, it is always advisable to avoid a flat look to the picture, particularly on faces, and to employ whatever light is available to add shape and contrast.

There are three basic lighting methods:

- key light
- fill light
- back light.

The key light is generally in front of the subject, illuminating them above the level of the background and is the main light source. In an interview situation this will create shadows to give the subject's face modelling and shape, the more acute the angle of the key, the deeper and more dramatic the shadows. In most cases you should aim for subtlety rather than any dramatic effect.

The fill light is a diffused light source from the opposite direction, filling in some of the darker areas and softening shadows created by the key light.

The back light is placed behind the subject, diagonally opposite the key light in order to separate them from the background and give a more three-dimensional look. Depending on the filming environment it may not always be possible to place a back light, but you should at least use a key light and a fill light to avoid a flat look and make the subject more visually interesting. And check that there is light in the subject's eyes, it makes them sparkle and brings the face to life.

Be resourceful when lighting scenes

Light can always be 'bounced' from reflectors or white poly to give a soft fill to darker areas, and gels can be used to give a coloured glow, or to cut down the amount of unwanted back light streaming in through a window. And you can always add an on-screen light, such as a candle or a standard lamp to create extra visual texture and mood.

If you are not lighting your subjects, consider how to make best use of natural light. You can avoid a flat look on the face by placing your subject near to a window to allow for some modelling on the features – though be careful not to put one side of the face too much into shadow so that detail gets lost on the other side.

The basic lighting kit

For a low-budget film you might consider taking along a basic kit comprising:

- ideally 2 × 800 watt, tungsten halogen (often known as Redheads) and 1 smaller 500 watt or 300 watt, tungsten halogen
- lighting stands
- poly boards, reflectors, gels and trace (to diffuse or soften the light)
- spare bulbs
- clamps
- extension cable
- gloves and duct tape
- socket tester to determine the safety of the supply. Use in-line RCDs to protect the crew from electric shock.

The Redhead is the basic workhorse of the film world and particularly ideal for close shots, whilst a smaller light can be used for highlighting small areas, or placing a highlight in a subject's eyes.

If you intend to film a performance – at a concert hall or inside a theatre or club – you'll need to consider how you might mix your own lights with the stage lighting. Apart from the fact that performers will not want extra lights shining in their eyes, the overall mood and look could become heavily compromised. Always work with the stage crew so that they understand your needs, and problems, so that together you can work out a solution.

Be alert for risks and hazards

And never forget the health and safety aspect of taking lights with you to a location. Hot bulbs sitting inside hard-edged metal casings placed on stands are a hazard to you, the crew and the public. Always allow bulbs to cool down before touching them and tape down electric cables, or place mats over them. Take an electrician if possible, but always have someone assigned to supervise any areas where lighting equipment is placed.

Consider alternative lighting methods

If in any doubt, or if you cannot afford lights, or do not have the room for them, you can always schedule your filming in daylight hours, making the most of natural light and using reflectors and poly boards to help take away any flatness to the image.

SOUND IDEAS

One of the most potentially neglected areas of film-making is the sound. On a shoot everyone generally pores over the look of the shot and its composition, whilst the sound recordist gamely endeavours to find a position where his boom pole will not be in shot or will not cast a huge shadow over everything within the frame area.

And when your rushes arrive at the edit suite either you, or a more experienced editor, will assemble the pictures, then balance the sound as best you can, without the benefit, as was standard practice in times of yore, of a separate sound mix in a specially equipped sound studio, under the control of an experienced dubbing mixer.

Sound should never be underestimated. It is a powerful force that can give a new and vibrant dimension to your finished film. You should be considering just how sound can enhance your story right from the moment you formulate your thoughts, through to the recce – where heavy ambient noise could be an unwelcome intrusion and difficult to deal with if not isolated – into the production phase, followed by the shoot and the edit.

Sound in practice

In practical terms you should use a camera that has an input for a directional microphone to give you much more control over the sound than a fixed mic, and a sound mixer such as the SQN-4S to ensure you can record a good balance with multiple sources without too much background noise interfering with the foreground. If filming a theatrical performance, check if you can take an output from the stage technician's mixing console.

You should record background atmospheres at every location to avoid unnecessary hicks and bumps in edits, or to 'fill in' sound drop-outs (such as lorry or aeroplane sounds cutting off suddenly in a dialogue edit), or to complement a scene; a gentle flowing river adding to the mood of a shot, background noises at, say, a fairground, to make the scene more lively. And when you schedule your shoot, consider what kind of extras might be worth recording to add an additional layer to the story, such as specially created background noises, prose and poetry readings, or songs.

Sound as a creative force

Remember how sound complemented the short film *Fester, Fester*, featuring two lads being pushed around in shopping trolleys to the sound of racing cars revving and screeching their way around a race track.

Or Rowena Cohen's *The Marvelling Lens*, a nostalgic film about Eugène Atget and his photographs of Parisian boulevards, shop fronts and spooky phantoms; the collection of still black and white photographs brought to life by lyrical music and the haunting street sounds of horses and carts, dripping taps and children playing on cobbled streets.

Or *The Hardest Way Up*, the documentary about the Annapurna expedition, where specially recorded sounds of crampons and ice-axes mixed in with light wind complemented the mute filmed material to give a feeling of isolation and breathtaking beauty to every shot of a mountaineer dangling on ropes above an otherwise threatening landscape.

To master the disciplines of sound as well as the visuals is to fully master the art of film-making; the combined strengths of picture and audio having the potential to create an exciting, fully rounded and formidable end product. The trick is to keep sound as an integral part of your thinking throughout the entire course of your production.

13

In the Hot Seat

For the majority of documentaries, interviews and voice-tracks drive the narrative, so how you approach your subjects and involve them in your story is of the utmost importance.

SOUND OUT YOUR CONTRIBUTORS

You should establish contact with your contributors as early as possible in order to ascertain their value to your film and to gain their trust. You also need to decide if they will be able to express themselves coherently and with enthusiasm, since dull, monotone voices attached to expressionless faces can sometimes do more harm than good, despite the worthiness or significance of what they are saying. Seek out people with strong, lively characters wherever possible, then isolate them in a one-to-one interview situation, away from the outside influences of friends and peer groups.

You should also leave them in no doubt as to their role in the production and how you propose to use their contribution within the context of the story. If they agree to be interviewed, but not on camera, you will need to seriously consider if their involvement is ultimately going to be worthwhile. Words alone are not enough in a visually inspiring story, where an individual's sadness, anger, triumph or dejection needs to be witnessed, even if only in fleeting moments, for us to fully appreciate their passion, euphoria, or despair.

Dispense information sparingly

You should be wary of giving out too much information to them in advance of filming, as spontaneity in their responses is vital. Obviously you need to discuss the purpose of the film and what contribution you hope they will make, but avoid handing them a list of proposed questions. There is nothing worse than rolling camera on the day and discovering that your subject has committed some carefully prepared answers to memory, resulting in a contrived, flat delivery, devoid of any emotion or fervour. Keep them informed whilst holding them at arm's length.

Establish an understanding with your subject

Sometimes you might find yourself having to go into an interview 'cold', without any preparation or advanced introduction. In such circumstances the relationship between you and your subject is likely to work more at a formal question-and-answer level than being a conversation between two people who have established a rapport. Unless you are grilling someone in an investigative situation, it is important that your subject appears at ease and feels you are someone in whom they can confide.

Even if it is not possible to meet up with a contributor several days in advance of the shoot (because it is too far to travel for a recce perhaps), it is always worth trying to arrange a meeting the evening before, or at least an hour or so before the planned filming session, so you can get to know them better.

MAKING YOUR INTERVIEWS VISUALLY INTERESTING

Establishing if your contributors have any photographs, home movies or documents to support the interview could well alter the proposed balance of the story if you know in advance that you can illustrate certain aspects of the discussion with material that might otherwise have been omitted. Watching a never-ending procession of on-screen faces delivering opinions, recollections and facts can be sudden death for a short film, because film is a visual medium and not a radio show. In certain circumstances – where you feel that a face reveals a concealment of the truth, or moments when someone is suddenly overcome with emotion – it is perfectly justified to allow the camera to linger. But don't overdo it. Variety and visual stimulation are important in maintaining audience interest.

Look for a background to film the interview against that will be interesting but not distracting. Neon signs, flashing lights, large blocks of readable text, hospital casualty entrances and areas where vast crowds gather should all be avoided, because it is not advisable to make the background more interesting than your foreground subject. Remember, too, that you should avoid any possible copyright issues that advertising posters, billboards, paintings, photographs or any blatant visual branding might create.

You should also consider if you can generate an interview environment that is pertinent to the story. Placing the subject in front of an appropriate background will certainly integrate it more closely to the narrative, even if you have to impose a certain level of contrivance. A member of a rock band sitting in front of an artistically positioned assortment of guitars and drums in a recording studio could be both interesting and relevant; or standing next to a stage as the rest of the band practise behind in order to add an element of fun as well as being appropriate – as long as the background is not too entertaining and the noise levels do not render the interview unusable. And bear in mind that even for interviews in an enclosed environment you can never have enough space for equipment, crew and lights.

Apply some lateral thinking

You could always approach your interviews with some lateral thinking. If your story is about a team of parachutists or skydivers, for instance, you might arrange for your interview sessions to take place inside an aeroplane that is on the ground inside a hangar so that the sound can be recorded clean. By filming hand-held and adding the sound of aircraft hum later at the edit, you can give the impression that your subjects are flying to a drop zone, adding more drama, immediacy and relevance to the scenario.

Alternatively, you could film hand-held walking alongside the contributor as they talk to you, describing buildings and vantage points, perhaps, or walking among members of a retirement home or youth club, meeting and talking informally to people gathered there. Film with two cameras if you want to add a further creative element, one close from the side, the other giving a wider perspective.

ELIMINATE DISTRACTIONS WHEREVER POSSIBLE

Avoid background clutter. Offices or rooms with polystyrene cups, progress charts, or paperwork scattered over desks can make your shot look tacky and badly thought out. And keep your subject away from walls or any flat surfaces that will not only look boring, but be difficult to light without casting unwanted shadows everywhere, and present you with an inability to back light.

And don't stand your subjects directly facing the sun or they will invariably start squinting, and politely ask them to remove any hats that will cause shadows to cover their face, or sunglasses that hide their eyes. As has often been wisely remarked, the eyes are the gateway to the soul.

Consider all the possibilities

If you were fortunate enough to make time for a recce you will already have identified any potential background sounds that could create unwanted problems. If your story is about a farm, it is not compulsory that you interview the farmer in the farmyard, with chickens, dogs and cows vying for attention. Take your subject to a nearby barn, or a field where you are away from the noise, but the farm can still be seen in the background.

Sometimes, it might be worth considering taking an interviewee to a high viewpoint, such as a balcony or a hilltop, where you can record relatively clean sound but still look down on a busy and vibrant background, for which you can record an atmosphere track afterwards. It is always advisable, whatever the ambience of the interview environment, that an atmosphere track is recorded for 'filling in' sound edits later.

Avoid recording in echoey halls and corridors, or rooms with background hums emanating from air conditioning systems or fans. If you identified them on the recce you should at least have had the opportunity to arrange for someone to turn them off for the duration of the filming. And try to film your interview in an environment that matches the scenes they will be inserted into.

Seeing someone working in a prison cell block and hearing tweety birds, or a waterfall, on the soundtrack may seem a little strange.

To summarise:

- Use photographs or memorabilia to bring the interviews to life.
- Choose an interview background that is interesting but not distracting.
- Choose an interview environment that is relevant to the story.
- Avoid backgrounds that could give you copyright issues.
- Apply some artistic or lateral thinking to the interview backgrounds.
- Avoid background clutter.
- Keep interviewees away from walls and flat surfaces.
- Do not put your interviewees directly in line with the sun.
- Remove hats or sunglasses that are covering their eyes.
- Avoid noisy environments.
- Avoid echoey rooms.
- Record an atmosphere track for use at the edit.
- Film interview cutaways after the main interview and *not* during it.

GETTING THE MOST FROM YOUR CONTRIBUTORS

On-screen contributors often become vulnerable when sat in a chair, facing a camera, with someone firing questions at them, so the more time you can prepare them and gain their confidence the better. Although most people these days are fairly knowledgeable about how films and television programmes are made, they are not always familiar with the various techniques employed to elicit responses, or how easy it is for a film-maker to distort – or give a false interpretation of – what has been said.

Your moral obligation to your contributors

Both the contributor and the audience rely on your honesty and integrity when you are conducting an interview on film, particularly when you later edit the story into a more concise representation of what was originally recorded. You may feel that if an interviewee has been lying to you, or given a false representation of the facts, you are justified in correcting the balance and revealing the truth.

Such matters often enter the arena of legal discussion, however, when lawyers and broadcasters get together to decide if such content can be screened. This is the case particularly if other people have been implicated in any accusations but not given a right of reply (or for which there is no firm evidence), or the interviewee might be called later to give evidence at a trial and the film, if made public, could be seen to prejudice the outcome.

In most instances people agree to be filmed because they have a story to tell, a point to make, or some information to impart, and there are no hidden agendas or ulterior motives behind their appearance. In such circumstances all they reasonably expect of you is that you outline your objectives so that they can co-operate and give their answers to the best of their knowledge and ability. In return, they expect a fair and honourable portrayal of the conversation that has been neither tampered with to their personal detriment, nor manipulated to fit conveniently in with your personal viewpoint.

And remember to agree any fees in advance before you run any tape stock, and make sure they sign a release form giving you permission to use their contribution.

IMPROVING YOUR INTERVIEW TECHNIQUES

If you want to get the best from your interviews, you should treat your contributors with respect, have empathy with their situation and be understanding of their viewpoint, even if you do not agree with it, whilst employing diplomacy and a variety of techniques to allow them to talk freely and uninhibited.

Avoid rehearsing any of the questions and answers before the camera turns, because they'll just end up firing all their barrels off-camera and you'll be left with a watered-down version that does not have the same impact.

Most new directors discover that interviewing people on camera is not as easy as it seems, their biggest mistake being to do more talking than the person who is supposed to be answering the questions. The interviewee is the star performer, not you, so it's pointless asking a question that is six sentences long in order to extract a reply of four words.

Make sure interviewees give complete answers

Firstly, you should explain that you need complete answers to the questions because your own voice will not be heard when the film is finally edited, therefore if they just answer 'yes' or 'no' it not only sounds like a reply, it does not give any actual information. 'Can you describe in your own words' is one way of extracting information. Repeating the question in part is another way to overcome the problem. 'Did you travel down to London by car?' might, therefore, be answered by 'I went to London by car because...'

Most people cotton on to what is required after three or four questions, but if not, you simply hold up your hand to stop them, give them a smile and start their answer for them. So, if you ask them 'When did you first realise you had a natural gift for playing the banjo' and they respond with 'At about the age of fourteen I suppose', you hold up your hand and say 'I first realised I had a gift for playing the banjo was when I was about fourteen...', smile again and signal for them to continue, at which point they will start the answer again, having been helpfully shown the way.

But don't be overly keen to jump in. Very often a contributor might realise their mistake and start again without prompting, or they might start the answer with an unusable sentence but then immediately give you an alternative 'in' point. So, if you ask them 'Has the drop in revenue made it difficult for the company?' and they answer with 'Yes it has, very much so. Fortunately we have a group of dedicated employees who'll make sure we don't fail...' they have clearly given you a clean edit 'in' point from 'Fortunately we have a group...' even though the start of the answer will be relegated to the cutting room floor. You also want to avoid the answers becoming formulaic when natural responses will always come across much better.

Listen to everything that is said

The trick is to listen carefully to everything your interviewee says. There will invariably be short gaps when they pause to gather their thoughts, but don't feel you necessarily have to interrupt or prompt them in any way. Often, pauses are part of the accepted reality of a reflective moment that will stay in the final cut – or your willingness to leave the interviewee thinking becomes a catalyst for their brain to move up a gear and to carry on giving you all that terrific stuff you'd been praying for but never thought would come.

Most importantly, never use your question list as if it is a prop. The questions are only a device, and a reminder, of the objectives of the film, but are not a script. When your contributor goes off at a tangent, and it's relevant, go with them. Listen all the time and show them that you are genuinely interested in what they have to say, following up their answers with questions that you may not have planned, but which are following their line of thought and opening up the story.

MAINTAINING INTIMACY ON CAMERA

A regular point of confusion for a contributor is where they are supposed to look during the filming. Quite simply, they look at you throughout the interview and not at the camera unless you specifically want them to look into the lens because it is your chosen filming style. If you do not make that clear their eyeline will dart between you and the camera and they will look decidedly uncomfortable and unsure of themselves.

Ideally, you need to sit as close to the camera as you can so that their eyeline is just off camera and their face isn't drifting into profile. Look directly at them as if this is a personal conversation between just the two of you, smile reassuringly whenever you can, and give them visual signs, such as head nods or thumbs up, to keep their energy and confidence levels up.

The main objective is for the interviewee to keep talking for as long as possible, without interruption, unless they begin to ramble, or repeat themselves, or start to go off course. Stop them if that happens, because it is far better to bring the interview to a halt momentarily rather than waste time and tape stock.

FILMING STREET INTERVIEWS

Interviews shot at random on the public highway – VOX POPS as they are sometimes called – are very different from those filmed in a controlled environment. People who are busy going about their daily business are often not happy with sudden intrusions into their lives, or they just don't have the time to stop and offer an opinion. On the other hand, it's surprising just how many gravitate towards a camera like a magnet the minute a film crew hit the streets.

If you are out and about grabbing street interviews you really need to be as mobile as possible, as in hand-held mobile, because setting up a tripod is not only time-consuming but potentially dangerous if the public are forced to walk around you. It is also difficult to manoeuvre people into ideal positions, such as using their bodies to shield traffic noise, or to take the sun (or shadows) off their faces if you limit your options to one static camera position.

How you phrase your questions is also critical in a situation where you do not have any time to explain that you need complete answers and not just 'yes' 'no' or 'maybe' and would they mind not staring into the camera. Basically you have to take control, so that they focus on you and answer in as comprehensive but concise way as possible before dashing off to buy that new pair of shoes.

Film a broad range of interviewees

Let's say you are making a short film about unrest within the local community caused by numerous recent council decisions – such as building a new leisure complex instead of a desperately needed health centre, or asking the public to pick up street litter because of a shortage of street cleaners – and you want to gauge local reaction. In order not to look biased, and to reflect an honest cross-section of opinion, you will need to talk to as wide a range of people as possible – setting up an interview, if possible, with a council representative, though you should leave that particular interview until last so that you can put some of the concerns voiced during the filming directly to them, giving them an opportunity to react in a positive way.

Get the public firmly involved

The public generally tend not to respond with any particular passion to situations that do not affect them directly, so your questions need to be phrased in such a way that they will feel the situation could impact on them at some point, even if they hadn't given it any serious thought up until now. A question like 'Do you think the council is doing a good job?' might provoke an angry and excited response in those who have a definite opinion, but it also offers a soft 'yes I think so' option to those who feel they are not involved in any way and have no particular inclination to be involved. Think of the topic under discussion as part of a large Circle of Involvement and you want to position the interviewee inside the circle, not standing outside it as a passive observer.

'What are the biggest concerns you have about the local council?' is a more positive approach because it focuses people's minds on the fact that there *are* concerns and perhaps they should consider how they might be personally affected. And just in case they need prompting you should always make sure you are armed with a list of contentious items to help provoke an animated response. 'How do you feel they affect you personally?' is the natural follow-up question guaranteed to put them firmly in the hot seat and invite a considered response.

Eliciting good reactions from people is not just about pressing the right buttons, but knowing when to press them. You should never approach people in an antagonistic or accusing manner, however, because of the risk of immediately alienating them. Better to employ tactical subtlety to place them in the line of fire so that they will feel uncomfortable about taking the easy route and pushing the responsibility for communal unity and participation on to someone else.

Keeping control over the numbers

Filming interviews in a street situation is difficult enough, particularly if there is heavy background noise or other distractions, but interviewing two or more people invariably compounds the problem. If you are talking to a couple, you will often find that one has more to say than the other and that person quickly asserts himself or herself centre stage. In such circumstances, it is better to frame for a single shot to avoid us seeing that the other person does not quite know where to look and is just standing there like a lemon throughout the course of the interview.

If the second person suddenly decides to intervene and have their say there is no harm in stopping and restarting the interview if you have been unable to reframe smoothly. A jump-cut from the single shot to the two shot is more likely to work than not. If three or more people are on camera you would be well advised to hold them in a group shot in order to avoid 'hosepiping' the camera from one to the other, invariably framing up on someone who has just finished speaking whilst their friend becomes involved in a heated exchange just out of shot.

Controlling children during interviews

And if any adults are accompanied by young children you will need to be extra vigilant, because children lose interest very quickly and become restless and fidgety. They will start imposing themselves noisily in order to gain attention, or take you to the very edge of frustration by waving brightly coloured lolly wrappers in shot, or munching on some particularly large and deliciously crunchy crisps.

You could always keep a bag of ripe, soft, juicy fruit on hand in case you can tempt the little menace into a temporary trade-off – but never underestimate the potential for kids to wreak havoc on your master plan, because there will be occasions when it's just better to be completely philosophical, put on a brave face, and quit while you're behind.

To summarise:

- Outline your objectives very clearly to your contributor.
- Do not rehearse questions and answers before turning over.
- Let the interviewee do the talking – not you.
- Get complete answers to your questions.
- Listen for edit 'in' and 'out' points.
- Listen carefully to what is being said and adjust your questions accordingly.
- Position yourself close to the camera in order to maintain a strong eyeline.

- During street interviews, angle your questions so that interviewees feel involved in the subject under discussion, aware of how a situation might impact on them.
- When filming couples, frame on a single if one of them is not contributing.
- When filming groups, hold a group shot rather than 'hosepiping' the camera.
- Try and find a distraction for noisy and fidgety children.
- Agree a fee, if applicable, and make sure a release form is signed before you leave.

14

On the Shoot

On a filming day, time evaporates faster than you would think possible, so the earlier you can make a start the better and you should be ready for all eventualities.

MAKE SURE YOU ARE FULLY PREPARED

Everyone involved in the shoot should know exactly where they are going, who they are meeting and what they are doing – either with a typed list of contact points at worst, or a detailed call sheet and maps at best – and should be attired and equipped for every possibility that the day might bring. Layered clothing is always advisable, so that you can adjust the layers according to changing weather conditions and temperatures.

Making a note of significant timecodes will make it easier to locate a shot if it becomes necessary to review it at a later point, so it's a good idea to carry some clear plastic bags with you – ideal for covering script or log notes if it starts raining. And a few elastic bands are also handy to stop your notes flapping about in the wind.

It is always worthwhile nominating someone to take production stills. When the film is completed and you want to market it, particularly if you are using any known actors, experts or presenters, photographs of the film in production will come in very handy.

ESTABLISH A SYSTEM FOR FILMING INTERVIEWS

When you created your shooting plan you should have scheduled your interviews at a particular location ahead of any complementary cutaway material. During the interview all kinds of things might be discussed that you didn't know about or hadn't realised were relevant to the story, but if you keep a check list you can pick up the cutaways whilst you are still at the scene.

If you are filming interviews yourself, you should still conduct them face to face in order to maintain intimacy, which means setting the shot first and then taking your position close to the camera. The main disadvantage will be the possibility of the subject leaning in and out of the shot; a problem remedied if you can connect a small monitor to the camera and place it just below your own eyeline for immediate visual reference. Another disadvantage will be the inability to zoom slowly in if the subject becomes emotional and you really want to get a lot closer to the face.

Employ creative thinking on composition

Interview shots should be varied anyway, so avoid the same size shot being held for interminably long periods. An ideal situation is to brief a camera operator on what you are looking for, leaving them to 'feel' their way through the interview and adjust the framing accordingly. With a monitor just below your eyeline you can see if there is a problem, or you would prefer a different framing, and restart a question if necessary after a quick reframe. Remember too that sound quality is critical. Place the mic above – and close – to the interviewee's face, and make sure that someone is always monitoring the sound input.

Consider if the shot could be improved by moving the camera back and filming the interviewee on a longer lens in order to make the background softer and separating it from the foreground to give it a more creative look.

And always have something with you to 'mop down' a contributor if they get too hot and sweaty. A basic powder compact will take the shine off of someone's face and make it a far more pleasant image to look at.

The rule of thirds

With interviews it is always advisable to observe the 'rule of thirds', which means that whichever side of camera your interviewee is facing, allow more space in *front* of their line of vision than behind, as the composition can look bad, or unimaginative, if the subject is either positioned exactly in the centre of frame or there is empty space *behind* them.

And think carefully about the distance you should leave between yourself and your subject. Sit or stand too close and it can become imposing, threatening even, certainly if they are not used to having a camera focused on them. Position yourself too far away and you could isolate them and make them feel exposed and vulnerable.

CONSIDER EYELINES AND SPATIAL RELATIONSHIPS

To explain this more clearly, let's look at a situation where you (or someone else) is interviewing a contributor and your questions will be used as part of the conversation. In this instance you may well film a selection of reverses of the interviewer for later insertion at the edit.

Such a situation would not be dissimilar to filming two actors in a drama talking to each other. The distance between the two actors is the Spatial Relationship that they both share and filming them requires a basic understanding of how eyelines work.

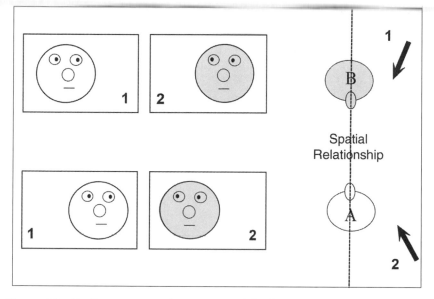

Figure 13   Eyelines – correct camera positioning

In this example, two characters, A and B, are standing opposite each other, the Spatial Relationship being the space that exists between the two of them. By drawing an imaginary line between the two characters and placing our cameras (1 and 2) to one side of it, we can create eyelines that will not confuse or disorientate the viewer when we edit the two corresponding shots together.

Camera 1, in this position, shows a close shot of Man A, with his eyeline facing just right of camera. Intercut with Man B's eyeline facing just left of camera, we will have created a visual flow to the edits. Note, however, that the top two shots have allowed for space **in front** of the eyelines, whereas the two lower shots have placed the space behind them, destroying the Spatial Relationship and causing the characters to 'bounce' between edits.

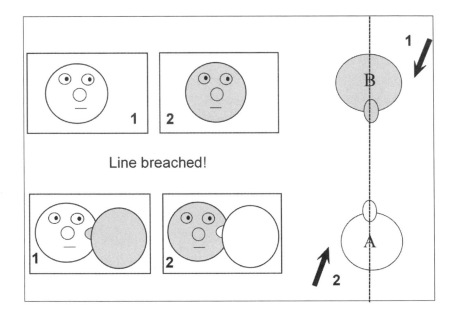

Figure 14   Eyelines breached

In this example, we have placed the corresponding cameras on either side of the imaginary line, resulting in the characters' eyelines now both looking in the same direction and giving the impression, when edited together, that one of them is standing behind the other and they are not facing each other. The two lower frames show what would happen if the corresponding shots were framed as two-shots and not as individual close shots. Not only are the eyelines both facing the same direction, but the foreground backs of heads are jumping position in the frame on the edits, adding to the confusion.

Many directors ignore these basic principles and use their experience to determine what they can get away with and what they cannot, but inexperienced filmmakers tread a narrow path between looking brilliantly innovative and technically incompetent, so understanding these conventions is an extremely worthwhile starting point.

Eyelines can become much more complicated the more characters you introduce to a scene, of course, and if you are not careful those characters will be looking about all over the place, with the audience soon losing all grasp of the geography between them.

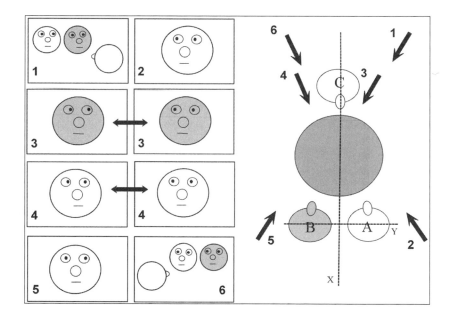

Figure 15   Eyelines

In this scenario, we have two characters in conversation with a third character sitting opposite them at a table. It could be a scene in a local pub for a drama or a drama documentary, or a meeting between three people that you are listening in on for a factual film. The imaginary line here is the vertical line marked as line X.

We will look at how the shots will cut between each other *in the order in which they will be edited.*

Shot 1 is taken on Camera 1 and is a three-shot with A & B's eyelines looking right of camera towards Man C, seen from behind.

Shot 2 is a corresponding close shot of Man C shot taken on Camera 2, with his eyeline facing left of camera – a similar situation to our first example, except that there are now two characters being intercut with the one character. Shot 3, however, initiates a change.

Shot 3, taken on Camera 3, is a close shot of Man B looking back at Man C, but he now looks from Man C to Man A, who is sitting, just out of shot, to his right. We need to cut to see Man A's reaction, but if we take that shot from either the Camera 1 or Camera 3 position, Man C's face will be in profile and will not match particularly well with Shot 3. The shot will also not be terribly dynamic if taken from a similar camera position, with a similar background.

To overcome these problems we simply place our camera in a new position so that we can cross-cut between Man B and Man A, and that new position is Camera 4.

But wait, you cry, *you've just crossed over the imaginary line X; the one you said we need to keep our cameras to one side of to avoid confusing eyelines!*

Well yes. And no.

Because we are now cross-cutting between Man A and Man B, the imaginary line X is no longer 'active', having been replaced by line Y, which is drawn between the two characters who are now having a conversation with each other. The cross-cutting between Cameras 3 and 4 now takes place to one side of *that* line, so no lines have been breached.

This particular scene segment ends on Man A looking from Man B, back to Man C, initiating yet another new camera position, Camera 5, because in order to now intercut between Man A and Man C, we have to shoot a *corresponding* eyeline, which means that Man C has to be looking to right of camera, and not to the left as he was at the beginning of the scene from the Camera 2 position.

When we cut from Camera 5 to a 3-shot on Camera 6, line Y becomes inactive, and is replaced by the re-activated line X. We are now effectively filming the interaction between the three characters from the *other* side of line X from where we started the scene, having crossed it, but not breached it. In this example it is the changes in the character's eylines from one to the other that has determined where the imaginary lines should be 'placed' and where the cameras should be positioned in order for the edits to work best.

DECIDING WHETHER TO USE TWO OR MORE CAMERAS

Although this scene could not have been filmed in real time because of the cameras appearing in each other's shots, deploying two cameras would be an option, although the conventional method would be to utilise one camera and reposition it for each set-up. In which case, of course, lights would be tweaked after each move and continuity of action and props would need to be closely monitored to avoid any visual embarrassments. You will also need to overlap the action on any change of angle and allow run-up and run-down time at the front and end of each shot.

In situations where you want stylisation or more control at the edit, particularly for structural balance and visual stimulation, you should consider filming bridging cutaways, or employing a variety of angles and frame sizes – most of which should have been worked out at the recce if at all possible. As always, good *preparation* is critical in order to achieve your creative objectives and to minimise the risk of over-shooting, particularly if two or more cameras are involved. There are many situations, however, where two or more cameras are essential in order to achieve best coverage: a concert performance, for example, or a town hall meeting where angry residents are responding to a committee's unpopular decisions.

Shooting on three cameras may mean deploying three camera operators, but because the operators will not be able to see the shots that the other cameras are taking, a full briefing will need to be undertaken so that each knows what shots they are covering, and the general framing for each shot.

In this scenario, someone is giving a lecture to an audience (Figure 16, opposite). Three cameras are used here, Camera 1 filming a mid shot of the lecturer, Camera 2 filming a wider 'master' shot with part of the audience foreground, and Camera 3 filming audience reaction. This gameplan would have been agreed before filming began so that each camera operator knew exactly the shots they were getting and how those shots would edit with the others. You could elect to use just one camera, of

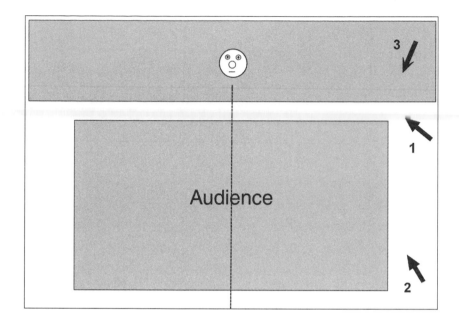

Figure 16   Lecturer and audience

course, filming the lecturer first and snatching audience cutaways at an appropriate opportunity, but your control will be significantly less and the end result will not be as interesting, particularly if there is audience interaction.

The imaginary line has been positioned between the lecturer and the middle of the audience, similar to the previous three-character scene. By keeping all three cameras to the same side of the line, the eyeline of the lecturer looking to *left* of camera will edit seamlessly with the audience looking to *right* of camera. If Camera 3 were to be positioned the *other* side of the line, the audience cutaway shots would change direction intermittently, upsetting the visual geography between the lecturer and the audience.

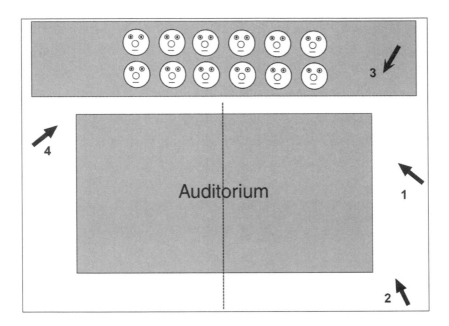

Figure 17   Group shots

If we replace the one person on the stage with several, we automatically create a situation where one camera cannot cover the action adequately. In this example a choir is giving a performance to the same audience, at the same venue, but an extra camera has been added so that we can obtain better coverage.

Camera 4 has been positioned the other side of the imaginary line in order to vary the angles; capturing faces that will intercut with choir group shots being taken by Camera 1. Disorientation is not such a problem cutting between Cameras 1, 2 and 4 if the shot sizes differ, and although cutting between Cameras 1, 2 and 3 would produce smooth edits, the edits between Cameras 4 and 3 would appear more disjointed because the audience cutaway shots would again change direction intermittently.

The imaginary line would become irrelevant if we were to make the choir, say, a gospel choir, and factor in audience participation with dancing, singing and hand-clapping. Shot variety would be of paramount importance, and we might even add a fifth camera position to capture audience shots looking back from Camera 4's position.

High octane filming of *any* kind requires a huge variety of shots in order to make it exhilarating and visually stimulating. When filming racing cars, skateboarders, boat races, windsurfers and theme park rides, you can almost never have enough shots to keep the excitement levels pumped up, so you need to be well covered to avoid running out of shots too soon at the edit.

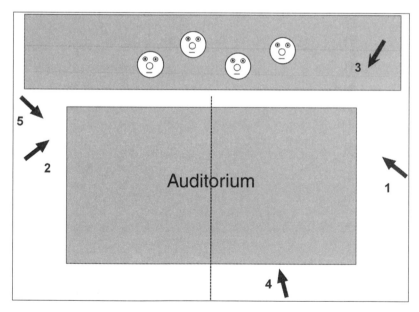

Figure 18   Rockband

The ultimate multi-camera gig is, not surprisingly, the rock concert; a non-stop frenzy of music, colour and lights that eats its way through shots of faces, guitars, drums, keyboards and gyrating audience at a startling rate. A full-blown television concert would utilise an abundance of cameras, from hand-held to tracking, from cranes to overhead pulleys and jibs, with every conceivable angle being covered. On a low-budget production you would be ill advised to contemplate a filming assignment of this magnitude with any less than three cameras, one static from the side, a second hand-held near the stage, and one taking audience reaction shots, and stage shots when required.

CONTROLLING YOUR FILMING RATIO

Possibly the greatest challenge for any new director is to make a film without their filming ratio going through the roof. In the previous examples where two or more cameras are needed to do justice to the sequence, you would need to plan the shots carefully and allow for the additional footage in your budget – and this does not just mean paying for extra cameras, operators and tape stock.

Whether filming with one camera or more, any over-shooting will impact on your post-production sessions, because the more you shoot the more you will have to digitise to the computer, the more you will have to log and store into separate files or 'bins,' and the longer it will take to assimilate and edit.

Be selective when filming documentary

On documentary it is not always easy to control the shooting ratio, particularly when something dramatic happens out of the blue, or interviews become more interesting and revealing than you had anticipated. In the longer term, experience will enable you to evaluate the worth of what you are filming as it happens, allowing you to be more discerning about what is important, or relevant, and what is not. You will also learn how to be more economical with your filming by editing the scenes in your head as you go, eliminating shots that are not entirely necessary within the bounds of your budget and schedule. The fact that you filmed a vast quantity of material does not mean that it will necessarily edit into a seamless and engaging story, so the trick, as always, is to plan as much as you can in advance and be as selective as possible on the day.

And always film a test, or check back your first shot of the day, to make sure there are no technical hitches before you carry on.

Decide on the best way to give dramatic impetus

Filming drama sequences invariably comes down to the director's personal approach. Some would prefer to cover a particular scene with a continually moving hand-held or Steadicam shot, whilst others might break down the filming into master shot, close, or mid shots and reaction shots. If you plan to film such a scene with a continuous moving camera, you should be absolutely sure before you wrap the actors or break from the location that you have the shot you want – because it may be too late afterwards.

In most instances it is safer to give yourself – and the editor – some options. You might also find that the actors will give you a better performance on certain lines on retakes, or you may have to lose a line in order to tighten the scene, both more controllable if filmed from numerous angles. You will also need to equate the set-up time for each separate shot with the time it will take to complete the scene successfully in one continuous move. Ultimately, it should be the shot that conveys the scene most effectively that you go for.

BRING YOUR SCENES TO LIFE

Never accept any scenes you are filming at face value; always look beyond the obvious to determine how you can film a sequence to make it livelier and more interesting. Audiences never view films from the same perspective as the casual observer who wanders into a situation. If you are walking along the pavement and you witness a car chase, it is from one perspective only; at ground level, with cars passing you at speed. On film, the action can be covered on multiple angles and edits; cars up and pass, interior car with anxious drivers glancing in wing mirrors, aerial or high angle shots, wheel shots, face shots, spinning tyre shots – all cut together at a frenetic rate to give a dramatic interpretation of exactly the same chase but designed to involve you more.

It doesn't have to be a car chase in order to make a scene lively and engaging though. You might be filming a day in the life of a youth club, where teenagers gather to play basketball, table tennis and badminton. If you are just standing in the hall watching them play, everything is moving through one single shot – your own line of vision. But if you put the camera on your shoulder and move in among the action, a perspective close to the table tennis net, inter-cut with action from the reverse side, perhaps, or following one of the players moving in on the basketball net, or ducking and diving with a team as they whack a shuttlecock backwards and forwards, you are bringing your audience into the action and involving them in the scenario so that they are no longer passive spectators.

Consider how the scenes might edit

If you are filming drama sequences, the script may already

indicate some dynamic edit points, such as a sudden and unexpected cut from a slow motion musical sequence of two people running through a cornfield to a baseball bat knocking a ball into the air with a loud crack, or a noisy street riot, or an express train thundering past camera. These kinds of transitions are as much a part of the texturing of a film as the pacing and content of the scenes themselves and show that the director has been applying some thought and imagination to how the material will be linked.

In documentary such dynamic editing points cannot always be pre-planned, but this does not mean they need be excluded. You could line up a shot that is momentarily confusing for the first few seconds, or let someone enter an empty frame in order to generate sudden visual energy. If you are filming someone stepping in, or out, of a car you might line up the shot so that the door slam becomes the cut point for the transition, or someone jumping with a heavy splash into a river. The combination of both sound and picture adds to the impact of the edit and, in some cases, sound preceding vision – such as the blast of a train whistle prior to the dramatic cut of it passing through shot – will enhance the effect.

Film scenes that will edit to best effect

If you film long continuous shots that you know will have to be cut down later, it is always worthwhile thinking about how they might be filmed to make the scene much more effective and dramatic. Two doctors walking hurriedly down a hospital corridor could be edited with a succession of jump-cuts that move the action on. In a similar scenario, you might even be able to repeat the action, with a walking shot from behind and a backward tracking shot from in front, in order to add an extra dimension to the scene. Make sure, though, that you have someone 'guiding' the camera operator for the front shot, and that both shots are filmed at the same pace.

Many scenes can, of course, be edited as jump-cuts at the editing session, but very often they will work better if you have pre-planned them. The timing of the edits is also important, however, because whereas the odd jump-cut might look like a mistake, a series of jump-cuts indicates that this is intended as part of the filming style.

SUPERVISING THE WRAP

When filming is completed at a location, never under-estimate the time it will take to derig: removing cameras from tracking equipment, taking down lights, actors having to remove wardrobe and make-up, wires and cables being rolled up, reflectors and poly boards being loaded back onto the van, rubbish being bagged and taken away, sets being dismantled, props accounted for and put away. Apart from the fact that you should be responsible about the condition you leave a location in, never forget that if any problems develop when viewing the rushes, you might just have to go back.

To summarise:

- Make sure you are fully prepared for the shoot and have left nothing to chance.
- Take production stills if possible.
- Establish a system for filming interviews, particularly if you are not operating the camera yourself.

- Keep a small monitor in your own eyeline for reference.
- Vary the frame sizes on interviews.
- Consider using depth of focus to make the shot more interesting.
- Keep a powder compact handy to 'mop down' a shiny face.
- Think carefully about your eyelines when filming drama sequences, meetings, lectures and performances at venues.
- Allow for more space *in front* of a subject or character's eyeline than behind.
- Decide whether you need two or more cameras to do justice to a sequence.
- Control your shooting ratio or it will impact on your editing time and your budget.
- Supervise the wrap and leave the location as if you had never even been there.

15

The Mechanics of Editing

It isn't so very long ago that film editing was the most widely used and accepted method for compiling shots and scenes into a meaningful narrative – its principles still form the foundation for the editing practices we employ today.

FILM ESTABLISHES OUR EDITING CONVENTIONS

The traditional film cutting room used no high tech equipment, just a picture synchroniser to run film and magnetic sound, with matching sprocket holes, synchronously over a workbench, with either an upright Moviola or flatbed Steenbeck on hand to either view cut sequences on, or to edit on directly. The only time this equipment ever needed attention was if a light bulb blew and needed replacing.

Logging shots was also straightforward, if somewhat labour intensive. Because each roll of exposed negative rushes from the camera had a series of key numbers imprinted down the side of the film, these numbers, placed at intervals of twenty frames on 16mm film, were automatically transferred to the positive print made from it. Key numbers corresponding to a particular shot, or a 'take', were written down so that the 'trims' for each shot – generally stored in rolls in film cans or hung up in trim bins for immediate access – could be quickly found if a shot needed extending. Needless to say, an assistant editor was generally employed to keep tabs on the day-to-day movement of picture and sound from film cans to workbench and back again.

The picture and sound elements generally arrived separately in the cutting room and the first job was to synch the rushes using a marked hand clap or clapper board as an identifying synch point. To maintain ongoing synchronisation with picture and sound as each element got sliced up and separated, a series of corresponding coloured ink numbers were printed onto the film and magnetic tape, and these too were entered into the rushes log alongside the key numbers.

Film employs basic but effective methods

The physical cuts to the film and its magnetic soundtrack were then made using a simple 'splicer', which lined the film up and guillotined along the frame line. The sections of film and sound were then spliced together with transparent sticky tape to make a 'cutting copy'. As work progressed and the edit took shape, shots and scenes could be quickly dismantled and reassembled by peeling away the tape and remaking the joins at the new edit points. It may sound cumbersome and primitive to today's programme makers, but it was a system that has worked – and worked well – since the early 1900s.

Whilst there were advantages such as not having to continually invest in new hardware and software, being able to hold the film to the light to see the images, and manipulating the elements manually, there were clear disadvantages. The film trims could easily get lost (often found hiding at the bottom of the trim bin) or the cutting copy became scratched, or the editor had to wait three or four days for any optical effects and transitions to come back from the film laboratory so that they could be cut into the edit.

The disadvantages of editing directly on film

And when the edit was finally approved, the cutting copy had to be sent back to the film lab so that they could cut the original negative to match the cutting copy using the key numbers to identify the cut points, and then produce a graded answer print for viewing and approval. Each subsequent viewing print then struck from the cut negative would be costly, and the only means of viewing the completed film was through a projector, with the sound being transformed into an optical track imprinted onto the film itself. After several viewings, the film could become scratched and dirty, or risk snapping or tearing, or becoming tangled up in the projection equipment.

It should be said, however, that film is still widely used today and many professionals prefer to edit their rushes together in a conventional cutting room using all the tried and tested techniques. Many have accepted, however, that whilst film retains a unique look, the modern methods for editing and distribution are more convenient and inexpensive. So, the general trend is for the exposed negative rushes to be transferred as digital files for grading and editing using the latest digital systems.

THE DEVELOPMENT FROM LINEAR TO NON-LINEAR

Curiously, the original video systems took the editing process a step backward when they were first introduced, even though the edits could now be kept spotlessly clean (apart from the odd technical dropout) and a computerised timecode system was employed to keep track of where the shots were stored for retrieval.

Although the impending technical revolution was clear for all to see, with obvious advantages, early analogue editing systems lacked the image quality that we have now come to expect, and the sequences were assembled as a linear edit – i.e. the shots followed one after the other so that you could only insert over them and not reassemble them unless each shot stayed exactly the same length. If you wanted to make any amendments or improvements to your edit you had to 'dub' the existing edit to another videotape roll, making the alterations as you went, but creating a less acceptable image quality because you had effectively dropped down a generation.

For all its potential disadvantages, film initially had greater flexibility in that you could shuffle picture and sound around to your heart's content, without any commitment being made until the film was finally neg-cut. For discerning programme makers it will always be the quality of the creative storytelling that is more important than the means by which pictures are shot and assembled, and early analogue systems certainly lacked the ability to give us complete flexibility and control over our material.

Digital computing software provides the solution

With typical resourcefulness and ingenuity the engineers and technicians who had worked tirelessly to provide us with a video alternative, found the solution in the form of digital computer editing. These random access systems basically allow us to retrieve and manipulate any section of our rushes and are the ultimate in non-linear editing – the electronic cutting room – complete with folders (or bins) to store clips in and an in-vision timeline to monitor progress as the shots are assembled, just as they could be on a picture synchroniser. The difference is that the original rushes are never cut up, destroyed or lost, but always preserved, intact, somewhere in the system.

DIGITAL EDITING COMES OF AGE

As someone who spent a large part of his career as a film editor, the arrival of video meant that I was one of the many dragged kicking and screaming into the latter part of the 20th century and generally resenting the arrival of the great impostor – but even I had to admit that this innovative fusion of technology and traditional editing methods was a giant step forward, and one to be welcomed.

The only drawback with the early non-linear systems was that they demanded vast amounts of storage capacity. With hard drives being relatively expensive, rushes had to be digitised at low resolution and edits made in a comparatively inexpensive offline edit suite before the master rushes tapes were then taken to a more expensive online edit suite with far greater storage capacity and state-of-the-art software, and autoconformed – i.e. a digital master assembled at high resolution by matching the master tapes to the timecode readouts (EDLs) created at the offline edit.

Digital editing as a dynamic new creative force

Today, non-linear digital computer editing is the popular, dynamic new force in editing. No longer do hard drives have to struggle to cope with storage capacity problems, as relatively inexpensive external drives can now hold extraordinary volumes of data, and with such dramatic improvements in digital technology, editors and directors can digitise their rushes directly into their own computers and work at high resolution, effectively by-passing the offline process.

Where Lightworks once led the field, Avid has been the professional choice for a number of years, with Final Cut Pro coming up fast on the inside lane and used by many professionals as well as beginners. Both systems have even introduced cost-effective software packages for use on laptops, giving greater flexibility to an art form that could only previously have been undertaken in a room filled with stacks of hardware, circuit boards, monitors and a couple of technicians.

There are numerous editing packages now available, even for the complete novice, from completely integrated systems down to software that comes bundled with a new computer (iMovie for Mac, Moviemaker for a PC), or independent systems you can buy, such as Adobe Premiere. Simply import your rushes to your computer, edit them and output the completed film as a digital file, or directly to DVD for inexpensive mass distribution.

DIGITAL EDITING IN PRACTICE

Each digital non-linear system has its own set of applications and buttons set out in different ways on the screen, each offering varying degrees of flexibility and complexity with regard to visual effects and control over both picture and sound balancing. The more you pay, the greater the range of gadgets-and-gizmos – but before wading in it is always advisable to first understand the principles of non-linear editing.

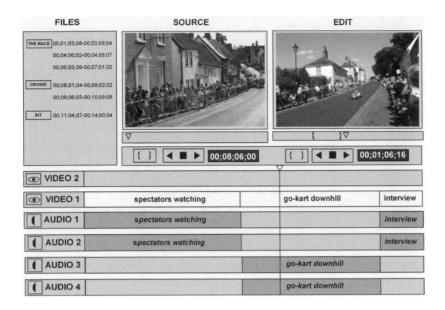

Figure 19   Non-linear edit screen (1)

A screen shot taken from any editing package will be far more detailed than the above mock-up, which I have used here to demonstrate the basics of how a digital non-linear system works. The digitised video files have been taken in to the system, broken down into separate sub-clips and placed in individual 'bins'.

In this example, all of the main race shots have been placed in a bin called THE RACE, the crowd cutaways have been placed in a bin called CROWD and an interview with one of the racers has been placed in a bin called 'INT'. Finding any of the scenes to edit, therefore, is simply a matter of scrolling down through the bins list and opening up the appropriate files from inside them.

In most editing packages you can go a stage further, identifying each of the separate shot files as, say, BLUE CAR MID-SHOT or YELLOW CAR CRASHES. The more time you take initially sub-clipping and describing shots, the faster your main edit will progress, not just for speed of finding them initially, but retrieving the shots when you need to extend either the picture or the sound, or both.

To view a particular clip you simply 'drag' it into the SOURCE WINDOW and set 'in' and 'out' points where you want the clip to start and finish (marked by the timecodes for that particular shot), then drag it down into the TIMELINE. As you can see, the picture lines up with its corresponding sound sections (Audio 1 being left stereo channel, Audio 2, right stereo channel), each occupying its own place within the Timeline. None of these sections is embedded into this position but can be moved around the Timeline at will, so that they can be placed either as 'locked' items (i.e. picture and sound together), or as separate items, somewhere else in the edit.

In some instances, you might place picture and sound for an interview into the Timeline, but then decide to replace the in-vision interviewee image with cutaway shots. You simply retain the sound section but delete the picture section and replace it with cutaway shots that you have found by going back to the bin files, viewing them in the SOURCE WINDOW and dragging them into the Timeline to replace the original pictures.

You can move the picture and sound elements around as much as want in the Timeline, because none of the settings will actually be locked into position until you 'save' the edit as a separate rendered file – and even then you can open it up again, make changes, then save it again – either with the same file name or with a new file name, so that the original edit is kept on the system just in case you need to refer back to it at any time.

As you progress, you can view the edit in the EDIT WINDOW, the timecode now indicating the accumulative running time. To change an edit, simply stop, re juxtapose, or replace, sections on the Timeline, switching between the SOURCE WINDOW and the EDIT WINDOW, depending on whether you are viewing and selecting from the rushes, or viewing the edit with the changes installed.

FLEXIBILITY AND CONTROL IN DIGITAL EDITING

In its simplest form, non-linear editing means that you place corresponding sections of picture and sound on a Timeline and bolt them together to make a running narrative. From then on it can become as simple or as complicated as you want it to be.

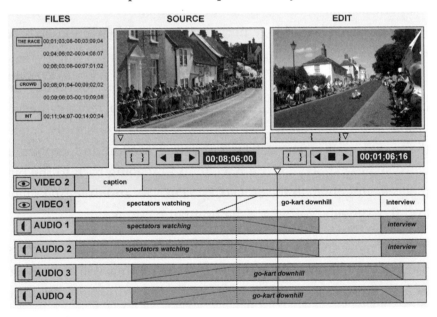

Figure 20   Non-linear edit screen (2)

This screen shot is from the same section of our edited film, the difference being that we have overlaid a caption in Video 2 and the two sections of picture – the crowd and the racing kart – have been extended beyond the edit point (marked here as a vertical dotted line) to allow for an in-vision picture mix. The sound has also been extended both sides of the edit point to allow for a fade-in and fade-out of the sound track in order to avoid any distracting hics and bumps and the outgoing go-kart sound has been faded into the interview section. We might also want to add some more drama to the story, so a separate section of excited crowd atmosphere – either recorded as an atmosphere track at the time or taken from a sound effects library – could be inserted into an additional Track 5 on the Timeline, and then faded in and out to avoid it bumping in and out of the edit.

Smooth transitions like this are the difference between a hastily put together edit that looks and sounds (despite all the hard work invested in the filming) like a home movie, and a more sophisticated edit where creative thought has linked arms with technical know-how to create a professional-looking end product. And be careful that the sound tracks do not start competing with each other; voices must be heard, clearly and coherently, above music and effects.

Take the time to understand your editing system

As with any system that you are unfamiliar with, you should spend some time getting to know how it works before you throw yourself in at the deep end. With non-linear editing the sky is the limit with what you can achieve – not just the juxtaposition of picture and sound, but the ability to alter the brightness and contrast, drain the colour, add diffusion, create special effects and so on.

Understanding the basics of editing and film grammar should always take precedence before you start getting involved in more complex creative technical dressing, so spend as much time as possible studying the documentation that comes with each system, even investing in one of the many day courses on offer at the various training establishments. It will be a worthy investment, because practice is ultimately the only way to truly master all that your chosen editing package can deliver.

ALWAYS CONCEAL YOUR BUILDING BLOCKS

As your film takes shape, your Timeline will begin to resemble an assortment of building blocks, which together comprise your narrative. Whilst you will be aware of all the audio/visual bits and pieces that have been placed on the various tracks to tell your story, this mosaic of moving imagery must appear completely seamless. There should be a reason and a motivation for every single edit that you make, and if your audience see or hear any of the various joins that you should have concealed, you will risk appearing technically incompetent as well as destroying the flow.

If you have jump-cuts in an interview, insert over them with a relevant sequence of images to complement the soundtrack and keep the viewer interested. Never cut in quick, snatched shots to disguise an edit, because the chances are you will just draw attention to a problem you have been trying to fix. Such clumsy attempts at misdirection generally misfire and should not be necessary if you planned your shoot properly.

Never leave your edits exposed; always blend your picture and sound in a co-ordinated symphony of rhythm, tempo and texture that makes each transition meaningful but invisible.

16

Piecing the Jigsaw Together

In film, whether drama or factual, you never show life exactly as it happens. Watching people swapping pleasantries with the postman, mowing the lawn, putting the rubbish out or doing the ironing are not the kind of things that compelling stories are made of, even though we all do them as part of the fabric of our day.

DISTILLING LIFE INTO DIGESTIBLE PORTIONS

When we write a screenplay, or construct a documentary narrative, therefore, we boil all the ingredients down into a compact but meaningful story, omitting the sections that are either irrelevant or uninteresting. To save time, money and effort, the planning stages of your film should have identified some of the elements that will have to be jettisoned, the filming process revealing many of the others. If you have not been able to steer a clear visionary path through the mass of possible content matter by the time you arrive at the editing stage, now is the moment when you will have to face up to that inevitable challenge.

Approach your edit with organisation and logic

Rather than be overwhelmed by the pile of rushes tapes overflowing with action shots you couldn't get enough of, or interviews that over-ran by several hours, take a deep breath and assimilate the situation before embarking on an editing frenzy without any plan of action. In all my years as an editor and director, I have never started an edit without first formulating a gameplan. Even if I had an actual script, I would still work my way through the document and mark off the appropriate takes to make life easier for either myself or the editor, even indicating where sections might be dropped.

CONSIDER CREATING A PAPER EDIT

If you did not devise a creative template for the shoot, it is not too late to formulate one for the edit, based now, at least, on the known elements that will comprise your story.

You could type up a progressive list showing how one scene might lead into another, or draw up a template just as we did in Chapter 10, showing action on the left and sound on the right. If it is documentary we know that it's unlikely to stay that way, because it is not until you cut shots and scenes together that you will really know if they work or not, and other, more interesting alternatives jump out at you, but at least it's a starting point and you have to start somewhere.

Working a logical flow through in your head and on paper gives you an opportunity to see the wood for the trees, with certain scenes forging a very clear link, and others not so clearly defined. If you are approaching your edit direct from the shoot, with all the scenes fresh in your mind, this exercise should be reasonably straightforward and you will discover, more often than not, that if a logical progression is not working on paper, there is a strong likelihood that it will not work in practice.

An independent video editor, coming to your story without knowing any of the content may, of course, throw everything up in the air and suggest an alternative gameplan – but it is always wise to at least make sure the spine of your story is in place before you start shuffling the deck around. You might even look at your paper edit and immediately see the possibilities for juxtaposition that had not been obvious beforehand.

Make timecode lists of relevant sections

Timecodes become a real asset as you start the digitising process. If you have filmed masses of interview tapes but do not have typewritten transcripts, sit and watch them through, getting a feel for where they work well and where they are not as strong as you previously thought, making brief notes of what is being said, with a timecode reference written beside each section. Such a list will become invaluable as the edit progresses.

Breaking the shots down into separate bins will help you assimilate further just what you have to play with, so that you not only reacquaint yourself with the material, but have it laid out before you with a stronger handle on where it is and where it might fit in with your current gameplan.

CREATE AN ASSEMBLY BEFORE FINE-CUTTING

Once everything is digitised, filed into bins and logged, the moment arrives when you can at last go into creative overdrive. Or can you?

You may well be chomping at the bit to give full vent to your artistic expression, but it is not always advisable to start fine-cutting and refining your scenes as you progress along the

Timeline. Not only do you lose sight of the big picture, but scenes you might spend hours editing into a mini masterpiece might not sit well among the other sequences and may even have to be dropped in the final analysis.

Letting go of amazing, breathtaking shots, or emotional tear-jerking scenes is one of the hardest things that directors and editors have to do – but the simple truth is that if they do not work within the final assembled narrative, they just have to go. And it doesn't matter if you risked life and limb to get that extraordinary shot of sunset over Hartley Wintney, or spent sleepless nights dreaming up a scenario that is guaranteed to win you a Bafta – if it doesn't work in the final edit, for whatever reason – it really has to go.

Take a disciplined approach

Many directors arrive at the edit suite with a very concise picture in their minds of how the entire film is going to piece together, complete with music and special effects, and want to start crafting the various sections into little jewels of delight without delay, but less experienced film-makers may not come with such a strong and complete vision, nor have had enough practice at honing their editing skills to know just what the possibilities are.

However well you think you know your material and how it might work best in the edit, it is often advisable to start with a basic assembly, laying the scenes down in the Timeline so that the story takes shape, steered by the interviews and voice-tracks that are driving the narrative. If there are any dull sections of interview you should remove them at this stage unless they are absolutely essential, and rethink areas that now seem laboured, muddled, not entirely relevant, repetitive, or clearly in the wrong place.

Think carefully about whether people, places and events have been set up properly so that the viewer can follow the storyline without confusion, and consider dropping any interviews for which you do not have – and cannot acquire – any footage to illustrate the interview or bring it to life.

EDITING AS AN EVOLUTIONARY PROCESS

The assembly should only be regarded as a stepping stone towards the completed film, because film-making is an organic process full of numerous alternatives and ever-changing possibilities that can be manipulated to tell your story in the most engaging way possible. For a drama you may already have decided to begin with a dramatic sequence to draw the viewer in. For a factual story you may have planned to start with an attention-grabbing opening pulled out from the middle of the story but dissected into two parts so that the first part becomes a cliff-hanger.

On the other hand, you may not have seen such possibilities and gone for a straightforward, chronological narrative. This does not mean it will stay that way, because in documentary particularly, things have a wonderful habit of changing in the telling. As the edit takes shape you may well see how to revise the structure so that it is completely non-chronological and much more exciting.

Build the elements step by step

With the spine of the story in place, take each section as it comes, working to make improvements at each viewing; trimming pictures, keeping action tight, making voice tracks more succinct, introducing music where it helps to quicken the pace or to make certain scenes more exciting or emotional. Then consider if you can move any of the scenes around in order to give them more impact, or to hold back information to make its revelation more dramatic, or to create or preserve subtext.

As the edit takes shape, be wary of allowing in-vision interviews to run for too long. Interviews are there for two reasons: to establish who is talking whilst verifying their credentials, because if someone is giving us an opinion it is only right that we know what qualifies them to express that opinion. And if a contributor becomes highly emotive it is human nature for us to want to share in that moment. If someone is being cagey and guarded we want the opportunity to make a valued judgement on whether they are lying to us or telling the truth.

Used wisely, an on-screen interview can have extraordinary impact, but keeping faces in an edit just because there was nowhere else to go will risk killing off your film long before it reaches its conclusion, since lingering on-screen interviews can sap the energy from a sequence and defuse the dynamics.

And never lose sight of the need to create light and shade in your edit; to keep the audience stimulated with changes of pace and mood, or unexpected revelations and turning points, all helping to ensure that your film does not run at one continuous level, but with multi-layered dips and bends; an engaging montage of picture and sound that keeps them enthralled from start to finish.

CREATING A HOOK

In a competitive marketplace, where producers and distributors are on the lookout for inspiring and inventive material, or television viewers run their fingers impatiently over their remote controls, your film needs to assert itself from the outset; to let the audience know that this is a story worth investing their time in; a story that has been thoughtfully put together and will not disappoint.

I once viewed a rough-cut about a police training academy that opened with new recruits singing hymns and being welcomed to the force by the commanding officer. Eight minutes in and still very little had happened other than a couple of induction talks and some training exercises, by which time the audience would have drifted away, with little hope of persuading them back.

The fact that there were several awesome scenes of high speed chases, attempted murder, stabbings and a major drugs bust were of little relevance to a viewing audience that had no idea such attention-grabbing scenes were on the agenda. Pulling up part of one of the action scenes to the front of the film not only created a breathless, dramatic opening, but established the kind of world that these raw recruits were about to step into, thus making us feel for their safety as they moved closer to real life situations, and increasing the dramatic tension from the word go.

Options and choices in devising a hook

The opening to your film does not necessarily need to be an explosive all-singing kaleidoscope of action and noise. It might be a long, slow, hypnotic pan across a desert wasteland, accompanied by a low whistling wind and tumbleweed drifting across shot – coming to rest on a man in a suit playing a white piano watched by a curious tribe of nomads who happened to be passing by. There is every chance the viewer will be fascinated by such an opening scene and be keen to know what is going on, happy to give you their undivided attention.

You may feel that the opening minute of your movie is so appealing that it draws the viewers in and keeps them glued to the screen until the final scene fades. On the other hand, you may view your edit and decide that, despite a strong opening message, it lacks the creative pull to hold the viewers' attention long enough for you to display the delights that they will eventually come to appreciate if only they could just be patient. Devising a creative template before the shoot could well have solved that problem, but if the material you have now pieced together is absorbing enough, there is invariably a way to use it to best advantage to draw the audience in.

Tricks and devices with your shot material

Mystery and intrigue are always guaranteed to hold someone's attention. Even momentary confusion or disorientation, providing you do not keep the viewer confused or disoriented for so long that they lose interest. The tricks and devices you can use are many and varied. Laying an eerie, mystical, music track in your edit at the start, for instance, accompanied by a montage of intriguing brief visuals from later in the film, with an interviewee's voice talking about a particularly chilling recollection is bound to rouse our curiosity; images of dark shadows in woods, for example, accompanied by someone talking about Seasonal Affective Disorder without us, at first, realising the alarming connection between the two.

Remember *Dream World* and the various nightmares people were having. Claire's car crash had initially been incorporated into the creative framework drawn up prior to filming, but even if it had not, one of the many dream reconstructions could be moved to the front of the edit to create a stark and immediate awareness of the depth of the problem that we, the viewers, are about to be exposed to. That is a far more interesting opening than an on-screen interview, or watching Dr Myers at work in his clinic.

To summarise:

- Assimilate your material before you begin your edit.
- Devise a paper edit.
- Make a timecode list of the various sections for reference.
- Put together an assembly before fine-cutting.
- Trim, tighten and constantly reassess your edit.
- Consider moving scenes around to give them more impact or to set up people and situations more clearly.
- Maintain light and shade throughout the edit.
- If possible, create an engaging opening hook.

Implementing any of the above does not mean that you are changing or interfering with the integrity of the story; indeed, in some instances, the chances are you are probably strengthening it.

This, however, may not always be the case.

STAYING TRUE TO YOUR OBJECTIVES

It is all too easy, when cutting your story down from, say, 12 minutes to 8, or 40 minutes to 30, to lose sight of some of your objectives. Not intentionally, perhaps, but because you have become so familiar with the subject matter you may not realise that certain important information has been lost in the distilling process.

Be careful not to distort the truth

Apart from possible crucial missing links and set-ups, the downside of trimming back your edit is either the misrepresentation of your interviewee's opinions, or a general distortion of the truth. Whilst shots and scenes can be manipulated to give greater emotional or dramatic impact, the manipulation of the truth should be avoided at all costs, because both contributors and audience put themselves in your hands to tell the story with honesty and fairness.

There will come a point, as with most edits, when you need to seek a second opinion; one that is far more objective than your own, because you are so welded to the material that you can no longer make a reliable judgement on whether the film reflects a clear vision, or whether it is delivering mixed or confusing messages.

Ask people to view your film who will give an honest opinion; people who will be able to make sensible observations and suggestions, allowing you to evaluate those opinions before making any final adjustments to your film. Then, before submitting it for general viewing, leave it for a day or two and review it, just to be sure that you are happy it has a strong structure and shape, has a natural rhythm and tempo, is well balanced and textured, is compelling, and fulfils all of your objectives.

Learn from your mistakes

Few new film-makers create a masterful work with their very first film. You may be happy with your final edit, delighted and relieved that it all worked out better than you had expected. Or you may feel that it could have been a lot better. The important thing is to learn from your mistakes and keep going, looking to improve every time. Craft and stamina are endemic in every fine film-maker, but craft is an acquired skill and one that can only come to you with patience and practice. In the long term, life experience itself will be the most important asset you will have in becoming a great film-maker.

17

Reaching Your Audience

When your film is completed you will obviously want people to see it, so where you target it will very much depend on whether you made it just for fun, as an experiment to test your storytelling abilities, to expand your knowledge and technical know-how, or to take a positive step towards working in the film and television industry.

It could be that you started out making a short film for your own amusement but discovered that it was an extraordinary journey of discovery and a rewarding experience. The film may even have developed into something far better than you had imagined, or has led you to make a second, more ambitious film that you want others to watch, either to promote as a showcase for your talents or for them to share the experience.

DECIDING ON AN OUTLET FOR YOUR FILM

Whatever your reasons for making your film, if you want to reach an audience beyond your close circle of friends and relatives, you'll need to consider the options:

- the internet
- broadcast producers and commissioners
- film festivals and competitions.

Uploading to the internet

The starting point for many is the internet. There are a growing number of websites exhibiting movies that have been made by non-professionals for general viewing, some on webcams, some generated by mobile telephone, others via camcorders edited as digital files. The first two will be of relatively low quality and, although the cheapest option, have the shortest life-span. They lack any real development possibilities within those formats because broadcasters require a certain standard of technical quality before they will transmit material. The individual websites will tell you the uploading procedure and their preferred formats, but generally these will be AVI, ASF, QuickTime (Mac), Windows Media (PC) and MPEG, most of which will be created automatically with the software that comes bundled with your computer. Apart from film, digital files generated on a computer will offer the best quality, dependent on the resolution and characteristics of your camera, and will look far more impressive. It is recommended that content originating from a DV camera or other high-quality source is, in fact, encoded at full frame size and a high bit rate on a format such as MPEG2.

Google Video (http://video.google.com) is open to content from film-makers whether amateur or professional, providing (like most websites) that the material is not pornographic, does not promote hatred or discriminate against any groups on grounds of religion, sexual orientation, or race, and the content does not infringe copyright. You retain copyright on the film you submit and no licence fee is payable for exhibiting the material, but if you are able to sell your work through Google Video you may receive a revenue share. By using the self-upload service, you retain complete control on how and when to distribute your film and can delete it whenever you want.

If you want to just upload a fun item of two to three minutes on YouTube (www.youtube.com), you simply create an account then click on Upload Videos in the right-hand corner of any YouTube page and enter information about your film, including its title and a brief description, then click on 'Continue Uploading'. You then click the 'Browse' button so you can browse your own computer files for the respective video file, then select the required file for uploading and click on the 'Upload Video' button. The upload time will depend entirely on the speed of your connection.

YouTube accepts video files from most modern digital camcorders in AVI, MOV or MPG file format. There is no limit to the number of videos you can upload, but there is a file size limit of 100MB for Standard account members, with no films or videos exceeding ten minutes. If you have a Director's Account, which is available to musicians, amateur film-makers and professional content producers, you can upload video files longer than ten minutes.

MySpace (www.myspace.com) also offers the facility to upload and exhibit your films and videos, and operates a similar system. Both YouTube and MySpace also have on-screen video tutorials to help with the upload procedure.

The film-making entertainment network community at www.My-MovieNetwork.com offers a facility to directors, actors, cast and crew to promote their work whilst enjoying videos, news and entertainment created by other community members. You can upload your films, create a unique portfolio to share with prospective employers and colleagues, find work opportunities, find others to work on projects with you, create a blog, post on forums, interact through private messages and connect users who work with you to your films and studio. In addition, the network constantly runs competitions, has industry news updates and members can upload images and create a personal profile.

THE NETWORK OF ADVICE AT YOUR FINGERTIPS

These websites not only offer an exhibition facility, but give you the opportunity to view other people's short films along with various interviews and advice from established film-makers.

The BBC's Film Network website (www.bbc.co.uk/filmnetwork) is a veritable goldmine of information, including a film-making guide and a people directory. The site offers the opportunity for you to view other film-makers' submissions, whilst dispensing information about distribution and film festivals, and informed opinion and guidance from established filmmakers. If you plan to submit a film for screening on Film Network, however, you should read the notes on the submission process, which differs from the other websites and requires you to send in your film on DVD and not as a video file.

FourDocs (www.channel4.com/fourdocs) is another hugely popular website, with a vast catalogue of short films available for viewing; video clips of established film-makers such as Paul Watson, Nick Broomfield, Molly Dineen and Penny Woolcock giving advice, a whole raft of video clips showing a range of production hints and tips, and the opportunity to upload a four-minute film to the site with the possibility of it being transmitted on Channel 4.

The British Documentary Website at www.dfglondon.com is well worth acquainting yourself with. Films can be nominated for listing in an extensive directory of films and film-makers, and the site has a host of film reviews, training information, as well as news of forthcoming events and film festivals throughout the world, seminars and workshops. For a small fee you can sign up as a member of the Documentary Filmmakers Group for special discounts and access to the DGF community.

Shooting People (www.shootingpeople.org) is a website dedicated to the growing community of active independent film-makers. It has a film calendar of events, a download facility for all kinds of film-making resources, a crew member database, interviews with industry professionals and a list of favourite film festivals.

TAKING YOUR IDEAS TO A BROADCASTER

There is nothing to stop anyone taking an idea for a project directly to a broadcast commissioner. If you have already made a short film that can be submitted as a pilot for a longer version, or even a series, so much the better. Broadcasters are generally looking for longevity and as many ways as possible to exploit a format, from interactivity on the World Wide Web, to DVDs, games and book publications. One-offs are rarely seen as cost-effective when set-up costs in design, sets, location fees, interviewee fees, narration, graphics, music and title sequences are utilised for just 30 minutes or an hour, instead of being spread over 13 or 26 half hours – and, for commissioners, viewer loyalty means higher ratings.

All of the broadcasters have commissioning websites where you can find out how to send in a proposal for a film or film series, so you will need to write up something that will either take their breath away or show really strong possibilities. And if you do submit a film to either a commissioner or a producer as an example of your work, it will need to be on DVD, so check that it is the preferred format – either PAL or NTSC – depending on which part of the world you are sending it to.

SUBMITTING YOUR FILM TO A FESTIVAL

Being realistic, your chances as a first time film-maker of having a film screened at the cinema are extremely slender. Back in the 1950s and 60s cinemas showed a B feature, then Pathé News or Look At Life, then maybe a short film, followed by the main feature. Today, audiences go to multi-screen complexes specifically to see the main feature, so a short film or documentary would have to be exceptional to find its way onto the big screen, especially on general release.

That said, organisations such as the UK Film Council operate schemes to seek out and develop film-makers who can show flair and innovation in work they have already completed, and various films the Council has commissioned have won numerous awards, including an Oscar. Cinema Extreme is one such scheme.

Whilst Cinema Extreme is not a scheme for inexperienced or first-time film-makers, many cinemas, film clubs and societies run short film events, and there are a multitude of international film festivals and competitions that you can submit your film to – many watched by industry professionals as well as the public. The British Documentary Website lists 'calls for entries' for forth-coming festivals worldwide and has a calendar detailing festivals for each month of the year. The BBC's Film Network website again offers excellent advice about film festivals, and the BFI at www.bfi.org has numerous downloadable information text files on its site.

Another marvellous resource you should explore is the British Council's website at www.britfilm.com, with online databases of films and film-makers, training and careers advice and a full directory of international film and video festivals. Exposures, the UK Student Film Festival (www.exposuresfilmfestival.co.uk) offers opportunities to new film-makers to submit entries for exhibition, the categories being Drama, Documentary, Animation and Experimental.

Without a Box (www.withoutabox.com) is a tremendous website to facilitate sending your short film off to festivals. You simply fill out one form and list which festivals you want your film sent to. Saves an enormous amount of head scratching.

Founded by Robert Redford in 1981, the Sundance Institute is a non-profit organisation dedicated to the development and exhibition of the work of independent directors, screenwriters, playwrights and composers, and the Sundance Film Festival, held each January in Park City, Utah, is widely recognized as the premiere showcase for international independent film. Whilst the Festival is geared towards the more experienced film-maker, its website at www.sundance.org/festival offers an interesting insight into independent production; the Festival having expanded over the years to include cultural film events, panel discussions, youth programmes, online exhibition and live music. Attended by more than 45,000 people from around the world each year, the Sundance Film Festival creates a vibrant, unique global community of artists and audiences, with streaming of short films and live Festival coverage, which embraces an international audience.

FINDING A DISTRIBUTION OUTLET

There are various distributors of short films who will take your work to international markets and try to sell it to broadcasters, airlines and other companies, but you will need to make a deal with them and provide all the necessary documentation to prove that you are the legal owner and have copyright clearances to sell your film on to a third party.

Shorts International (www.britshorts.com) manages the world's largest and most diverse film catalogue devoted to short films, available to all territories in all genres, and film-makers are invited to submit their films on DVD for consideration. The organisation will, however, expect exclusive distribution rights over the licensing period.

The Independent Cinema Office (www.independentcinemaoffice.org) is a national organisation that aims to develop and support independent film exhibition throughout the UK and works in association with independent cinemas, film festivals, film societies and the regional and national screen agencies, and includes a detailed list of UK film distributors.

Future Shorts (www.futureshortscom) has created a rapidly expanding network that allows film-makers the opportunity to have their work seen on the largest theatrical platform worldwide, from just one submission, at its own monthly worldwide film festival.

Organisations such as The London Film Academy (www.londonfilmacademy.com/courses) offer one-day courses, for example *The Business of Film* and *Marketing and Distributing Your Short Film*, along with a whole series of events and screenings for film students.

Going it alone

You could always write to organisations and corporations to see if they would be prepared to sponsor or part fund a project, based perhaps on a short film example you can send to them. Broadcasters these days are far more open to sponsorship possibilities than they used to be, though you would need to check individual company's guidelines.

Or you could promote your film on your own website – and other people's websites – to purchase and download directly, or explore niche markets that you might be able to sell to. An enterprising colleague recently made a documentary about the scooter community, took a large box of DVD copies to a scooter festival on the Isle of Wight and sold them directly to an entire army of scooter enthusiasts. It's surprising what can be achieved some-times with just a little resourcefulness.

USING YOUR FILM AS A STEPPING STONE

It is unlikely that the first film you make is so successful it propels you into the fast lane at turbo speed. The competition is massive, but every short film you make moves you further along the road, and never underestimate the bargaining power that experience – and a growing network of contacts – could eventually bring. At least you can show people that you are prepared to invest your own time and money in a project and that you have a genuine passion for film-making. At the end of the day, confidence and commitment count for a great deal and making a series of relatively inexpensive short films is certainly a way for you to discover your shooting style and help you determine what kind of films you want to make, moving you closer to the one that will ultimately single you out. As with most things, the best way to learn is by going out there and doing it.

Economy of distribution

Most modern computers will allow you to transfer your digital computer file directly to DVD via a built-in DVD writer, but if it doesn't have one you can always connect an external DVD writer to your USB port – which means you can copy your film as many times as you like for a few pence a copy, and distribute them to a limitless number of producers, commissioners, film festivals and independent companies.

Keep your foot firmly in the door

If you have serious aspirations to work in the film and television industry, contact some of the film training schools to see what courses they are running, and apply for any of the jobs that at least will get you a foot in the door. Many websites list job opportunities, for example www.broadcastfreelancer.com and www.mandy.com, the former charging a small fee for registration, the latter being free for a weekly email listing.

Creating imaginative movies and then being pro-active in alerting other people to their existence is one sure way to push yourself into the open. If you are tenacious enough, someone somewhere will eventually take notice – and you must never sell yourself short when it comes to marketing your skills and your talents. Bear in mind, though, that film-making is for long-distance runners and not sprinters, and is a lifetime's journey of discovery – so take every opportunity to improve your education in the craft of film-making and what it can offer to both you and the people who will watch your films.

18

New Frontiers

Only a brave person would dare predict what communications tools we will be using 20 years from now; but the most effective tool we will always have is our imagination and it is most unlikely that the art of storytelling will change significantly.

Some of the most innovative film-makers of the past 100 years have produced amazing works with precious few resources and with relatively unsophisticated equipment. Yet their endeavours have opened our eyes to the world around us, influenced our perceptions of people and events, and presented us with the means with which to continue informing, entertaining and finding enlightenment for the many millions who will share our planet over the next 100 years and beyond.

It is important we do not get misled into believing that the emerging technologies of the twenty-first century can create instant and sustainable magic at the touch of a button, or turn us all overnight into Schlesingers, Spielbergs or Scorseses. True storytelling does not require spectacular frills, tricks or devices to delight and enthral us, and compelling narratives that stay the course can only be produced by those who have real dedication and passion for this most illuminating and rewarding of occupations.

Ingenuity, tenacity and craftsmanship will continue to be the driving force as emerging film-makers forge new frontiers and take up the challenges set by their predecessors – not just by displaying creative resourcefulness, but by approaching their work with an abiding sense of responsibility. In this way, film and television and all the complementary technologies will continue to play a crucial role in our lives and, in doing so, remain as relevant in the future as they have in the past.

Picking up a camera and expressing yourself through your own short films could be the first step in playing an inspirational and meaningful part in that future.

Further Reading

For those keen to progress their skills, Focal Press have been providing an excellent range of essential books on film and video production for a number of years, including *Directing: Film Techniques and Aesthetics* by Michael Rabiger, *The Visual Story* by Bruce Block, *Writing the Short Film* by Patricia Cooper and Ken Dancyger, *Filmmaking Fundamentals* by Nicholas Proferes and a variety of books on the techniques of film-making, from cinematography and sound recording to lighting, television production and film and digital editing. See www.focalpress.com

Other books that provide an excellent insight into various aspects of the film-making process include *Story* by Robert McKee, *Adventures in the Screen Trade* and *Which Lie Did I Tell?* by William Goldman, *Directing Actors* by Judith Weston, *The Pitch* by Eileen Quinn and Judy Counihan, and three extremely comprehensive reference books, *The Guerilla Film Makers Handbook*, *The Guerilla Documentary Makers Handbook* and *The Guerilla Filmmakers Movie Blueprint*, all three available at www.livingspirit.com

Index